Looking for Love

in the Sears Catalog

Beverly Leach

Looking for Love
in the Sears Catalog

Beverly Leach

Arena Press
Grass Valley, CA
2014

Published by Arena Press

Email: beverlyleach@gmail.com

This edition was produced for on-demand distribution by lightningsource.com for Arena Press.

Cover design: Maxima Kahn
Typesetting: Wordsworth (wordsworthofmarin.com)
Editorial Support: Molly Fisk
Editor: Ariel Amlin
Technical Support: No Problem, Local Computer Service & Repair
Front and Back Cover photos: Family archives

Some of the names in this book have been changed for reasons of privacy.

© 2014 by Beverly Leach (Ruth Ghio)

All rights reserved. No portion of this book may be reproduced or transmitted in any form or by any means, electronic or mechanical, including photocopying or recording, or by any information storage or retrieval system, without permission in writing from the publisher.

Printed in the United States of America

ISBN 978-0-9894958-9-9

Dedicated to my parents,
Edna and Ralph Leach,
and
Ruth Lambert, my grandmother.
Without these people there would be no story.

I also dedicate this book to my Finnish relatives and ancestors who played a larger role in my development than I ever imagined.

I also wrote this book for my four children:
Kathy, Charlotte, Beth and Tony,

who were also affected by this story and may never have known
what in the hell was happening?

CONTENTS

INTRODUCTION	9
Chapter 1: ORIGIN OF FINNS (1860–1932)	13
Chapter 2: ORIGINS OF THE LEACH AND HEATON FAMILIES (1800–1932)	25
Chapter 3: BIRTH (1932–1935)	33
Chapter 4: NORTH DAKOTA (1935–1937)	39
Chapter 5: THE NORTH DAKOTA YEARS (1932–1937)	46
Chapter 6: THE TRIP (1937–1938)	57
Chapter 7: PORT ORFORD, OREGON (1939–1940)	65
Chapter 8: WHEELER STREET, OAKLAND, CALIFORNIA (1939–1943)	73
Chapter 9: WHEELER STREET AND LIFE OUTSIDE (1941–1944)	81
Chapter 10: THE WAR (1941–1945)	91

Chapter 11: ROLLINGWOOD, CALIFORNIA (1943–1945) 97

Chapter 12: HARBOR GATE, RICHMOND, CALIFORNIA
    (1945–1950) 109

Chapter 13: HIGH SCHOOL, FRIENDS, AND WHEELER
    STREET (1945–1950) 121

Chapter 14: GROWING UP, LEAVING HOME
    (1946–1950) 133

Chapter 15: CONCLUSION 145

ACKNOWLEDGMENTS 151

INTRODUCTION

There was once a child watching the snowflakes fall, pile softly,
Mounds upon the prairie and covering the rare tree.
She looked to the grey sky in wonder and awe!
She tumbles rolls in the snow
Pulling her sled, daring the highest hill.
Shouting, playing loving the white world.

Dr. Irving Yalom, a famous psychiatrist who taught for many years at Stanford and was a practicing psychotherapist who has written several books, once said, "Every life is worth a novel." I believe this to be true. Perhaps that is why I decided to write my story, perhaps I wanted my children to know their roots, both the dark and the light, and perhaps because like all stories some of it still intrigues me and puzzles me.

For years, friends suggested I write my story, especially my friends who shared classes with me in the psychology department at Chico State University. It was still a time when knowing one's self counted. In my mind I did not see what there was to write. Some of the story embarrassed me; some I never wanted to reveal and some of it overwhelmed me.

In later years, I compared my story to the stories of my friends who were world travelers, authors, adventurers, who had more degrees than I had ever imagined possible, who spoke elegantly and were highly successful in their fields. Now, *they* had important stories to tell.

Often in the year I was working towards my Master's degree, we all told our stories many times. It was then I began to value life stories. Since I listened to the most compelling stories from all kinds of people, young and old, those who lived in the same house all of their lives, those who moved often, married often, and then those who stayed married to the same person for their lifetime. The stories were as varied and as rich as the complexities that make up the human psyche. It was during this time I knew that living a special kind of life did not necessarily make for a more interesting story than the story of the housewife who stayed home, cooked, cleaned, did the laundry and got everyone out of the house in the morning. There was a unique richness in living a daily life and specialness about every person's inner life. What beauty!

When I attended a workshop with Joseph Campbell and Stanley Keleman, one of them said, "The hero's journey is daily life." I don't think either one of them was responsible for the quote, but I have learned from listening to the many people who have crossed my path the truth of that statement. And so I decided to write this hero's story about living an ordinary, often extremely challenging and hard life, but as I often say, "Hard does not mean bad."

I began writing this story when I got my second Master's Degree. I was in my sixties. The program was at Holy Names in Oakland, California. It was a special program, " Culture, Creation and Spirituality." A main theme in the program was "The Universe Story." I am still quite clear that every story, the tiniest to the most magnificent, contributes to the development of this larger than our imagination story, "the story of creation." Our lives add to the nuances, the puzzles, the questions, the answers and all aspects of the evolution of the Cosmos. Now it is some twenty years later and I have decided to finish this story until this point, which I consider the last part of my journey here on earth, but certainly not the last part of my journey.

We all share something in common in our varied stories. In every story I have heard over the years, I could find some part of my story. We all come from the same cloth, but we each represent a different piece of the cloth. We are connected through the threads of the cloth. Our story, woven into the cloth, gives it a particular kind of beauty.

Chapter 1

ORIGIN OF FINNS
(1860–1932)

Early morn, dark, nothing, snow pressed against the window
Darkened house.
No light, exciting, scary, Oh! What fun.
An icy tunnel from the house to the barn.
The tunnel cold dark, following her father, the flashlight
Where is she now, a child of awe and wonder?

I was born in the Fred Finch Home for Unwed Mothers in Fargo, North Dakota. My mother was of Finnish descent. They were pioneer immigrants who homesteaded and farmed the land in and around two very small towns, Wing and Arena, North Dakota.

Each of these towns had one main street, and probably a total of six to ten houses. My grandfather had a bar in Wing; there was a small grocery store and probably a church, which I don't remember. At one time I believe it had a Finnish Temperance Hall. The grocery store in Arena was closed and the building was abandoned. There was a two-story brick school. My father helped build the school and then attended it as I did. There was a small post office, where my grandmother was postmistress, a German Lutheran Church that did not welcome Finns, and most important, the grain elevators bordering the railroad tracks When I returned some fifty years later to Wing, all I saw was an old folks' home and all around, nothing. In Arena, the post office was still there as were the church and the abandoned school waiting to be torn down. In the school yard, partially hidden by the tall grass was the old teeter-totter, now obsolete. As a five-year-old child, I had loved that teeter-totter. A school yard piece of equipment too tame for today's children.

My grandmother, Olivia, was born in Cokato, Minnesota. Her last name was Saari. Her father, Johan Petter (Niemi), came from Sala, Finland. Her mother Brita was born in Haaparanta, Sweden, a city located on the Swedish-Finnish border. As the story goes, sometimes the city belonged to Finland and sometimes to Sweden. There is still family in Finland and the family has been traced back to the 1500s. Distant relatives still live in the Arctic Circle and in the area closest to Sweden. According to the story, my great-grandmother's house was moved to the outdoor park in Helsinki, since the Tartu Peace Treaty between Russia and Finland was signed in her home. It was the treaty that freed Finland from Russia and allowed Finland to become a country. Whether the story is true or not, I cannot say. It became part of the fabric of my history and it also became part of me when it was told over and over again.

My grandmother was one of three children. She had a sister and one brother. From what I heard when I eavesdropped on the grownups in my family, it was not a very close family. Her sister and she were hostile to each other. I remember her sister coming to visit once. I do not remember it as a very pleasant visit.

Olivia was an exceptionally intelligent woman, who hated housework and all the chores associated with maintaining a home. She had four daughters and four sons. The oldest was a girl, Ethel, and then all down the line the children alternated: girl, boy, down to my youngest uncle, Norval.

Ethel took over the running of the household, I imagine, long before she was a teenager. She was soon joined by the next daughter Florence and they became the tyrants of the homestead.

These two older sisters treated my mother, the third girl, like a servant and were both cruel and vicious to her.

Olivia favoured her sons over her daughters. Many years later when the family lived In Oakland, California, I remember hearing her tell a lie over the telephone when my youngest uncle had cut school. He was nowhere near the house, but as far as the school was concerned he was home sick in bed.

While still living in North Dakota, she spent her time working in the barn helping with the animals, maintaining the garden and working in the fields. She was not high on nurturing skills, but I think it is safe to say none of the Finns I grew up around were high on nurturing skills or emotional availability. My mother's oldest sister, Ethel, actually raised the younger children, which would include my Aunt Evelyn and my Uncle Norval

Grandfather Elmer's family came from an island located in the Gulf of Bothnia between Finland and Sweden. The island, Hailuoto, was twenty-five miles long and eight miles wide. The original name of the family was Procko. Eventually there were so many Prockos on the island they began to call them Juniti Procko, which soon was shortened and became Juntilla, which became Josephson. Grandfather Elmer's father was Abraham (Juntilla) Josephson. The name was changed when they came to America. Depending on when you were born you could be either Finnish or Swedish. My grandfather claimed to be Finnish. He spoke, read and wrote Finnish. His Finnish language skills were excellent, so excellent, he became the lay minister for the Finnish Lutheran Church in Berkeley when he was in his sixties or seventies. If you know anything about the language you know what a feat that was.

Finding the origin of the Finnish language has been a challenge. It seems most closely related to Hungarian. Finland did not have a written language until sometime in the mid-eighteen hundreds when someone translated the Bible into the Finnish language. When I would look at the Finnish newspaper my grandfather had mailed to himself from Minnesota, I was always curious about a word that might have four "k's" in a row and other strange combinations of letters. I was shocked to learn that when you pronounced a word in Finnish, every "k" was pronounced. I practiced with little or no success.

My grandfather's mother Anna was born in Paulanka, Finland. The Swedes used the Finns for "cannon fodder," explained one of the guides when I visited Finland. This tension, prejudice, and abuse followed them to America. In North Dakota the Swedes and Germans defined the culture and the Finns remained second-class and unwanted citizens until the Second World War. In spite of our nation's reputation as a place for anyone, the real truth is that wherever you look in the United States people were not welcomed by the people in the areas they chose to live: in Boston, the Irish immigrants; in New York, the Jews and the Italians; and in the midwest, not just immigrants like the Finns, but also the natives who were here long before we were. In California, it has been the Chinese, the Japanese, the Mexicans. I cannot think of a place where those who were viewed as different—maybe just because of religious beliefs, the darkness of their skin, the strangeness of the language they spoke, or their different ways of living everyday life—had an easy time. Sadly it has not changed much, or perhaps more accurately as much as I would like. My oldest daughter is a lesbian. My son-in-law is African American, East Indian and Native American. My racially mixed grandchildren and my new great granddaughter whose father is also African American are all people I love. I want all of them to feel loved, valued and accepted by their neighbors and their community. I am not forgetting the slaves of the South. That history and story still needs deep healing, as do all the stories here. I suppose when we seriously heal the story of slavery, all the other stories will benefit.

I do know that some of my grandfather's family still lives on an island between Finland and Sweden. The story that the town hall burned down in the sixteen hundreds is the reason the family cannot be traced back to an earlier time. Is it the gospel truth? Well maybe it is, or maybe not. It is one of the stories I heard most of my life.

My grandfather was one of twelve children. There were six girls and six boys. At least three of his brothers homesteaded on adjoining land. His sisters were more scattered. One of his sisters married a Banttari boy from Minnesota, also Finn. They had sixteen children. They named their oldest, a girl, Limpe. Until I grew up I thought she was the youngest and they had run out of names. I pronounced her name as "Lumpy."

My grandfather's family was very religious. They were Lutheran in their religious orientation, but any resemblance to conventional Lutheran doctrine was purely coincidental. His six sisters were by far the most fanatical. In spite of this orientation, my grandfather owned the only bar in Wing. I hung out in that bar and was fed ice cream bars by all the patrons until I got really sick of them and never wanted one again. Most, if not all, the patrons were relatives.

The six sisters believed in faith healing. Two of them died at a young age because of their refusal to see a doctor. One died of tuberculosis and the other from breast cancer, as I remember the gossip I heard around town and the bar and on the homesteads. The gossip followed us to California until they had died. They not only opposed doctors and dentists, they opposed pretty things, like home decorations, colorful clothes, make up, all bodily adornment including hairstyles. They opposed anything that might be fun: dancing, games, music, and cards. They believed in work. Any deviation was considered the work of the devil.

My grandmother did not follow these beliefs or teach them to her children. She was quite disdainful towards my grandfather's sisters and their belief system. She was much more of a free-spirited, bright, creative woman than her sisters-in-law. Her children were condemned for their lack of devotion and for practicing and engaging in the ways of the devil. My grandfather actually supported his wife. But when the surrounding countryside judged them as sinners and as evil and as doing the devil's work, it was a challenge for any of my mother's family to find their place. The young men were often let off the hook and their acting-out behavior was accepted as the norm, after all they were men, and what could you expect. It was the wife's job to tame them and my grandmother was doing a terrible job of taming her husband. As a result of this religious tyranny, my mother, her sisters and her brothers were never able to resolve their conflict around religion. This rejection and judgment of the family along with the prejudice of the surrounding community left the children in my mother's family with deep anxieties, a sense of never really belonging, hurt and anger that were played out in alcoholism, isolation and a stoic, sometimes mean nature. The men were alcoholic and had fun. The women were judgmental, fearful and often cruel to one another. Everyone was competitive and loved to tease and demean each other.

My grandfather's family was politically active. They were liberals and radical in their thinking and political beliefs. One of my uncles and several cousins were card-carrying Communists. My mother hated and denied this story, which is most likely true, since it was the reason given my brother when he was in the Air Force and was denied a security clearance. It limited his opportunities for advancement.

Another family story is about my grandfather's mother, Anna, who was emotionally unstable and always difficult. What this is saying is she was in worse shape than her emotionally unstable family. After the death of her husband it was decided she would live with each of her children for one month in each year. However no one could tolerate her and so she often did not last a month in any one household. There were bitter fights among my grandfather's six sisters about what to do about their mother. I don't know if this was ever resolved or if she just died in the midst of the bitterness and ongoing conflict.

As I have stated before, the Finns were culturally discriminated against. This discrimination ended because of Finland's diligence in paying back their World War I debt to the United States in the 1930s. The Finns were quite proud of this fact. When I visited North Dakota sometime in 1997, we visited the Finnish cemetery outside of Wing, North Dakota. My great-grandparents contributed the land. The local Lutheran churches were mostly Swedish or German and would not allow Finns to be buried in "sacred ground."

As a people, the Finns are very quiet, shy, withholding, stoic and rather somber. I once watched a program about Finland where the government held dances for single men and women in the hopes of encouraging more marriages. A woman who sang at these dances was asked if the Finns had any complaints about her. Her answer, "Yes, they did. They complained I smiled too much."

When I was in Finland one of our guides, an Irishman, told us, "Finns went to the sauna every Friday night, drinking vodka until they were drunk. Finns do not drink socially, but to get drunk, then they go back to a bar and fight. Usually someone gets killed." I imagine that may have changed some. In my own family the men in the family drank to get drunk. I believe this was also true of my aunts, except they did not drink as often as the men.

My mother was the fifth child of eight. She was the third girl. The oldest Ethel was in charge of the house and was basically considered an "Old Maid" all the time she lived in North Dakota. She married Jack, her first husband, shortly after moving to California. All my family loved Jack. He was especially good and kind to all of us kids. My youngest brother adored him and he adored Roy. Ethel and Jack never had a child of their own.

After Ethel came Ervin, who never married and seemed like a rather strange guy, living with his parents until my grandfather and his second wife died. After their death he was hospitalized in a mental hospital. I overheard my mother and her sisters talking about it. One of the stories about Ervin was that he was a "peeper" as my brother put it. It seems he was a "Peeping Tom." It is likely he was caught and institutionalized rather than sent to jail.

Then came Florence who was considered the family beauty and tomboy. All the local boys were smitten with her. When Florence was a preadolescent, my grandmother made her canvas underpants since she was always tearing her clothes. The stories of her beauty were legendary in North Dakota and when I visited people were still asking, "Is she still as beautiful as she was as a young woman?" She married a man from out of the area. They never had any children.

Then came Harold who was considered extremely brilliant. He was married once and ended up abandoning his wife and child. He was an alcoholic.

My mother Edna was next. She was a sickly child who had polio, diphtheria, and several cases of pneumonia. It was often feared that she would die. When my mother was diagnosed with polio, my grandmother made her walk and kept her moving. She would also cover her legs with hot towels. When the doctor finally arrived at the house, brought there by one of my mother's brothers, he announced that my grandmother's treatment had most probably saved my mother's life and prevented her from being crippled. My mother told me of overhearing her parents talking once when she was sick about how they did not expect her to survive the night. My mother had many stories of sitting at the top of the stairs eavesdropping on her parents.

After my mother came Leslie who also abandoned his wife and child. He was an alcoholic. He died in Chicago from complications from both diabetes and alcoholism. He had both his feet amputated and died in a home for indigents.

Then came Evelyn whom the family called Elma. She was the only one in the family to graduate from college. She has two children and three grand children. She is now in her early nineties. Her husband Cal passed away about a year ago. Evelyn believed he had saved her and I think he did. She is the only living member of that generation. She lived a very different life than any of her family. She was an elementary school teacher. She travelled all over the world, had enough money to live in a manner none of her family were able to accomplish. Her husband managed the money to make sure they would have ample money until they died. She was a master at bridge and golf. Evelyn and Cal moved to an assisted living facility and I saw Evelyn last year. Her husband Cal had just died. She can no longer see or hear well enough to do many of the things she loved. She is also a diabetic. She has written two children's books. She is very proud of this accomplishment. Her grandson Adam illustrated both books.

Somehow my grandfather escaped and never had diabetes. He died at eighty-six. He once told me he was ready to die. "I have had a good life. I have raised all my children and I am ready to die." I was shocked and yet I understood. He felt he was done and he could leave the planet now. When I mentioned this to my mother, she just scoffed and did not believe me.

The last of my mother's siblings was her brother Norval. Evelyn was about eleven years older than I, so Norval must have been about nine years old when I was born. He became an alcoholic and diabetic. He drove truck all his adult life and had wanted to be a truck driver since he was a boy. He had four children. His oldest son drowned in Lake Comanche when he was about twenty. His two other sons live in the Bay Area and Cottonwood. His daughter lives in Colorado. Her husband committed suicide. Her daughter also has passed away from drug abuse. Arlene, my uncle's wife, is a Native American and is still alive.

My mother was an exceptionally brilliant and creative woman. Her two older sisters Ethel and Florence tormented her and made fun of everything she did or attempted to do. In an order to avoid their teasing and judgments, she made her first dress under the bed when she was seven and sewed the dress completely by hand. How she did this is still a mystery to me. What I do know is she made beautiful clothes for me and never used a pattern. I would describe my mother's family as competitive, cruel, often mean and vicious in their interactions. They were mean-spirited and took great delight in teasing and making fun of people. Three of my mother's four brothers were alcoholics and the fourth one was very strange. My brothers hated him and avoided any contact with him. My youngest brother Roy called his uncle Ervin a pervert. None of my brothers would ever discuss their feelings towards him. My mother and two of her sisters have also struggled with what I could call bouts of alcoholism.

My mother's stories told of having ink spilled on her clothes, or a gift of perfume dumped out in the outhouse and of being constantly teased because she was not blonde or fair. Both her older sisters would deliberately not set a place for her at the table. Neither of her parents ever said a word until she retaliated and left a place bare for one of her older sisters, Ethel or Florence. When that happened she was sent from the table without food.

Her brothers were all bright, talented men who remained laborers and rarely accomplished much, with the exception of my mother's younger brother who remained a truck driver all his life in spite of his alcoholism. Two of my uncles abandoned their children. I raised one of these children myself. She is my oldest daughter.

Of the eight children only one graduated from high school; Evelyn, the youngest girl finished her schooling after the family moved to California. She was the only one to graduate from college. She attended the University of California.

The last child, her brother Norval, attended school in Oakland after the family left North Dakota. He would have been in about the seventh or eighth grade when the family arrived in Oakland. When he began high school, I believe he attended Oakland High School. I doubt he ever graduated. He was often truant. I believe he joined the Army rather than continue in high school.

While the family lived in North Dakota, attending high school was a challenge. The family homestead was a farm outside of Wing, North Dakota. The closest high schools would have been in Arena and Bismarck. The only way to attend either high school would have been to board in someone's home. There were few places in Arena to work for board and room.

Transportation in the winter was tricky at best and nonexistent at worse. Since access to a high school was a hardship, most of the time high school kids roomed with families in Bismarck. To add to the complications, everybody was often needed to help run the farm. Girls were less needed and therefore had more opportunity to attend high school. Even though there was a high school in Arena, it was too far from the Josephson farm to make attendance easy. After moving to California, my youngest aunt and uncle had more opportunities. All of these exceptionally bright young people did little with their intellectual capacity. For my mother this lack of opportunity contributed to her suffering. She was a brilliant, creative child who grew into a brilliant creative woman with no opportunity to really use her gifts. It was a family story.

It was with my mother's family that I had the most contact as I was growing up. Their lives were characterized by chaos, conflict and unbounded acting out. Some were religious fanatics. My mother's participation in and response to all this confusion greatly influenced me. She needed something from them she could never get. Her fear and anxiety was palpable; it was always present and always an influence in our lives.

The Finn story historically is one of a people treated badly by their neighbors, living simple and often superstitious lives. Not only did they suffer from prejudicial attitudes and mistreatment, but also they themselves were often competitive, bitter, judgmental, mean and violent with each other.

When I was in my early forties, I decided to contact as many of my mother's sisters and brothers as I could find. Aunt Evelyn, my mother's youngest sister confirmed my impressions of her family. Until she met her husband, the family called her Elma. When she brought her future husband home to meet her parents, her brothers and visiting cousins all lined up at the door, laughing and joking, making fun of her and her future husband until they arrived. Then they straightened themselves and with exaggerated solemnity shook Cal's hand. When they left, they had a field day laughing and making fun of Cal and Evelyn.

Her brothers made her life totally miserable with their endless teasing. Her parents never took a stand for her or stopped the cruelty. Behind her back her sisters jeered and made fun of her. Her husband refused to have any relationship with the family and insisted she use her given name, Evelyn. I don't think my aunt ever completely recovered from her childhood. I think her husband finally convinced her she was a valuable person.

When I contacted my Aunt Florence, my mother's second oldest sister, about my birth, this was her reply, "What did you expect us to do, welcome her home with open arms so she could go out and do it all over again?" I don't remember all my conversations with my mother's siblings; I do remember they rarely had anything good to say about each other. My oldest aunts were particularly mean about my mother.

Chapter 2

ORIGINS OF THE LEACH AND HEATON FAMILIES (1800–1932)

Cold trembling tired child fingers hurting from the cold.
Tears stained red-cheeked face, crying, pleading for care.
No answer, no response — alone the child stood.
Now I know where she has gone.
Hiding deep, afraid to ask for loving care.
Dear frightened girl will you ever come out and play?

My paternal Grandfather Grover Leach is less well known to me. I know he was married and divorced at least three times. He had a younger brother, the same age as his son, my father. In 1997 this brother died. This is really the only story I know about Grover Leach's extended family. I never met any of this family. Again there were several children. Grover's nickname was Slim. I suspect he was called Slim since he was very tall and very thin.

My grandfather and I did not meet until I was seven years old. He abandoned my grandmother and my father while in Alaska. He left her for another woman. He married this woman and had several more children. I have met three of my father's half-sisters from this marriage. None are now alive. Slim left his second wife, when she began to go blind. He left her for another woman, Ollie.

He had only one child, a girl named Sandra, with this woman who is my father's youngest half-sister and is about the same age as my youngest brother. My dad maintained contact with both of his surviving sisters until his death. After his death, my brothers and I lost contact with them. Slim was married one more time after being married to Ollie, Sandra's mother.

Slim was a telegraph operator for the railroad as a young man and all his life he was a gambler, sometimes professionally, sometimes not, but always compulsively. His self-centeredness and lack of regard for any one's needs except his own is revealed in the following story:

When Slim was twelve years old he was out hunting and accidentally shot himself. An Indian found him. The Indian took him to his home, where he nursed my grandfather using herbal remedies. He was able to keep him alive. This unnamed Indian and his treatment saved Slim's life. His parents posted signs around the countryside about his disappearance and offered a reward. The Indian saw the notice and returned my grandfather to his parents. He was taken to the Mayo Clinic and, as the story goes, he was the first child admitted to the clinic. He was the center of attention and was fussed over and, as my mother said "spoiled rotten." He remained in the clinic for one year. In the accident he had shot out over half of his stomach and had a hole in his chest that looked like a large crater and a smaller crater in the side of his face. His mother was warned to be careful and not overfeed him. However, she was so grateful he was alive she could not say no to him and allowed him to have all the food he wanted. Consequently, he ended up back at Mayo Clinic and was there for another long period of time.

As devalued in North Dakota culture as my Finnish ancestors were, my paternal grandmother's family was esteemed. Her family came to North Dakota from Iowa. My grandmother is buried in Iowa.

My great-grandmother was French and may have had some English and German blood also. She was a staunch Methodist and a leader in the temperance movement in North Dakota. My great-grandfather was English and German. He was a Methodist who, according to my father's cousins, never agreed with his wife's religious beliefs but simply "let her have her way." She was much more rigid and dogmatic in her religious beliefs than he was.

There were eleven children in this family. One son, Russell was killed in the First World War. He and his brother Vinton went to the battlefields of France. Russell announced to his mother that he would not be back, but Vint, his brother, would. Vint was the family nickname for Vinton. When they landed in France, Russell was shot and killed as they climbed the first hill. Vint did come home and lived until his seventies. He was diabetic as was his son Patrick. Patrick died shortly after his father. He died during surgery with complications related to diabetes. Vint was the person in my father's family that I knew best. Both sides of my family have a history of diabetes.

My Great-aunt Neva moved to New York where she was a designer for Saks Fifth Avenue. She never married but was thought to have been a mistress to someone in New York. She was quite interested in the occult and in spiritualism. I know little about the other children. According to my mother, my grandmother, Ruth, and her two sisters, Neva and Edna were "loose women." Or as my mother put it, "They had round heels." I know nothing about the other girls in the family. I don't remember their names and don't remember ever meeting any of them.

I did know my father's Uncle Jake, his mother's oldest brother. He had a passel of kids and was well known in the countryside. Jake had over fifty grandchildren when he died. His daughter, Mary has forty-nine grandchildren. Until his death, my father was the oldest surviving cousin.

In my first trip back to North Dakota after leaving some fifty-six years before, I visited the original farm owned by my great-grandparents. I went to a family reunion with my parents and my brother. My father's family still lives in the original house and continues to farm the land and raise pigs. The house was as I remembered it, except they had added a bathroom, but the old outhouse was still standing. When I visited twenty-five years ago, the barn on this land was the oldest standing barn in North Dakota. The strangest part of the trip was to see how much I resembled my father's family in appearance and in body structure. Most of that family continues to live within commuting distance of each other. My cousin, who lives in the original house, lives across the road from his parents who farm the adjoining acreage.

This family was also active in politics but in a much more conservative way than the Josephson family. My great-grandfather served one term in the State Assembly. In general his family was a traditional well-thought-of farm family in their community.

My father was the first baby born in the Bismarck Hospital. At six months he had not gained any weight from his birth weight. My great-grandmother had my grandmother's brother, Vinton, milk all the cows for a sample of their milk. She held each glass of milk to the light to determine which one was the richest. She selected one and the milk of that particular cow was mixed with a barley gruel, which she fed to my father in a bottle with a large hole until he began to thrive. It is hard to believe my father survived. My grandmother's milk must have been just strong enough to keep him alive but not strong enough for him to thrive.

My father also went without adequate food when he and his mother were deserted in Alaska. They returned to North Dakota by train by way of Denver. She had no money and both she and my father went hungry for three days. She divorced my grandfather and eventually married Frank Lambert, who loved my father, bailed him out of trouble and was the only father he ever really knew.

Frank was my grandfather and was always generous and kind to my mother and to all of us. When he died everyone for miles around owed him money. He supported his community and his family in the best ways he knew. He had lost an arm in a threshing accident and I remember my curiosity about his empty shirtsleeve.

Upon returning to North Dakota and marrying Frank, my grandmother became postmistress at the Arena post office. My father grew up in Arena. The family lived in the newest, most modern house in Arena. The house was on a hill away from the rest of the town. Behind the main house were the washhouse, the icehouse, the barn and a chicken coop. The washhouse was most often turned into a bathhouse with a shower and a sauna. In the winter ice was cut and hauled to the icehouse, a building partially underground. Straw was packed around the ice and on top of the ice. Root vegetables, apples, grains, smoked and dried meat and sometimes fresh meat was stored in the icehouse. Everything put in during winter froze and was preserved.

My father often visited his grandparents' farm. Until he died he still had fond memories of these visits. Sometimes I think he was sorry he ever left North Dakota. By the age of nineteen my father had a serious drinking problem. He shared with me that the first time he drank he stayed drunk for three days. Most of those days he was blacked out.

These stories of my family of origin help me to understand who I am. I believe that these families are deeply embedded in my cells and have influenced me in deep and mysterious ways. My father was deeply spiritual and had returned to his Methodist roots. He was a man of deep feeling. All of this combined to make him often overly sentimental and emotional. I believe my father's struggle with alcohol was a perverse way to contact his own spirit. Like his father before him, he was self-centered and neglectful of his family and his family responsibilities. I had more of a connection with my father than I did my mother. I considered my father a very good man, who was unable to grow up and take responsibility for his life. Over the years I have recognized that in may ways he remained an overindulged child, but I got more attention from him than I ever got from my mother. He did not like children and even with his grandchildren he was often impatient and intolerant. He was better with age, but never really warm with any of his children and grandchildren, except my daughter Elizabeth and my brother's daughter Rowena.

My mother was determined, self-centered, bitter, angry, and cruel. She also was bright, gifted, creative and innovative. She sewed beautifully. She made all my brothers' suits, her own clothes and mine as well. She re-upholstered the furniture, made lamps, tore out walls and always maintained a beautiful flower garden. However, she was emotionally unavailable, unable to nourish or to have an empathetic response. I don't ever remember her crying, or a time when she reached out to make physical contact. She was emotionally unstable and had periods when her fears would turn into paranoia. When I saw the movie, *Like Water for Chocolate*, it was like watching my own mother's life. Yet it was her strength and determination that kept the family from going hungry and she maintained some form of shelter for us. I recognize more and more how my mother's family also lives in me and has shaped and formed me. This is the history out of which I came. The early memories that stand out for me are the times when my father was so drunk he could not walk. One of these times he was walking along a barbed wire fence falling every step or two with my mother watching him from the window yelling, "He's going to kill himself on the barbed wire." The second time was when he fell down the long flight of stairs from the back porch to the basement. I remember him grabbing for the rail and pulling it down as he fell from the top to the bottom. My mother was standing at the top of the stairs screaming and immobilized.

The third incident happened one night when I was about three years old. I walked out of the bedroom to witness this scene: My father had a gun and was standing on one side of the dining room table, yelling he was going to kill my mother, then all the kids, and last himself.

My mother, looking totally terrified, begged him, "Ralph, please put the gun down, go to bed get some sleep, everything will be better in the morning."

I began to yell at him, "Stop! Stop! Please stop." He looked at me and threw the gun at the dining room window, smashing it. At that moment I remember the feeling of the child in me leaving. In the place of this child a pseudo-adult began to develop, a crust of maturity, an act of competency. The primary task of my childhood was simply to survive and to help this terribly hurt family survive.

I knew very early that it was to my advantage to keep the family together. It was clear to me that if my mother raised me alone she would destroy me and if I were left with my father he could not provide for even my basic needs, or at least this is how I saw it in my young child's mind. To survive I became very alert, watchful and hypersensitive to the moods of those around me. I began to take care of the family and assumed it was my responsibility to keep the family together and to make sure we all survived. I also became very interior and quite hidden. I worked at being invisible and lastly I turned to nature for my nurturing and for my connection. In a very personal sense the earth became my mother.

Because of the circumstances of my birth, I was often teased and made fun of by other children. Children ran away from me and hid from me. I was isolated and excluded from play. The stigma of my birth was well known in the little farm community where I lived the first six years of my life. Nature became more and more important to me. It was where I felt at home, on the prairie among the grasses, the flat land, watching a sunset, the clouds, the wind and even the rain. It was a long time before I understood why I was so generally mistreated in those early years.

I believe those early years gave me a relationship with the dark and the shadow that influence much of how I saw the world. It has been both a blessing and a curse. I am more comfortable with my shadow than most people and I do not hate it. In fact, I am more and more accepting of the oppressor in me, the cruel parts of me, the Hitler in me and all those parts that are often considered "bad" or unacceptable. I have created a relationship with those parts in order to humanize them and to learn to love.

My parents' marriage united two very different cultures. Both of these families brought together their creativity, brilliance, diversity, pain, grief and dysfunction to create a new paradigm in the hopes of creating some kind of opportunity for healing. I believe this was my paternal grandmother's hope. Both families had deep spiritual roots in the land, in the plains. My mother's family brought the mystical traditions and rituals of Finland and my father's the Methodist heritage of his mother's family. Together this formed my spiritual heritage. I have worked to accept all of these varied and sometimes conflicting parts of myself. I believe we all have an opportunity to transform our family history and heal the wounds of not only the past but the future as well. Sometimes I have experienced transformation in an unconscious way and sometimes in a conscious manner. I do not consider my mother a bad woman and over the years I have learned to be more understanding of her pain and been able to develop both love and empathy for both of my parents. It has not always been easy and there are times when I still lose my tender feelings towards them. They were and remain difficult people in my life, even though they now are both gone.

Chapter 3

BIRTH
(1932–1935)

There was once a child who watched the snow melt.
Exposing new grasses, leaves budding on trees.
She touched the pussy willow's softness.
She looked up at fluffy white clouds, lambs, dancing ladies.
Strange faces moving, ever changing shapes, stories to tell her.
Her deep loneliness created her world.

Years ago in a workshop with Joseph Campbell and Stanley Keleman, I wrote a fairytale about my birth. I included it in the play I wrote and now here it is again.

Once upon a time there was a poor farm girl who had two wicked sisters who abused her. They called her names, gave her the most menial tasks to do and found all the ways to make her see herself as ugly. They called attention to anything they could and called it a flaw. Even at the dances they would jeer at her and make fun of anyone who danced with her. "You don't want to dance with her, look at her fat legs and see how dark she is." They ruined her most precious possessions and tore up her things.

One time the handsomest, most sought after man about town asked her to dance and took an interest in her. She began to dream dreams of a new life for which she hungered. She deeply longed for the "good life." For her it was not the life of the farm or the life she knew. Her dreams carried her into the world of Cinderella.

But as fate would have it she found herself with child. The man was shocked and unbelieving. After all didn't all the wise women of the land agree that a maiden could not get pregnant the first time she had sex. They had been together only one time. He fled to another land and left her to face the future alone.

Her wicked sisters finally found out the truth, told her mother and father. The sisters shamed her, jeered her more and forced her out of the house even though it was the middle of winter and the land was very cold. Secretly her mother found her a home in a distant city.

At the home, her dreams shattered, she waited the birth of the child. She was puzzled by the pregnancy that shouldn't have happened and was frightened of not finding a home for her child. She was confused, angry, hurt, and felt guilty and overcome with shame and hopelessness. The baby was born and she began to look for a place, a home for the new girl child.

One day she received a letter from the young man's mother, whom she did not know and had only heard about. This woman requested to see the baby. She had a glimmer of hope while she awaited the arrival of the child's grandmother.

Upon seeing the child the grandmother asked her to wait. Again the young woman replied, "I only want a home for my baby." She repeated her wish over and over to the grandmother and she waited.

The grandmother pondered the situation on her return home. She had never had a daughter. She had only a son who wasn't going to school or working consistently, who was drinking too much and developing quite a reputation as a ladies' man. He was self-indulgent and indolent. "Where would his life end," she asked herself. "Perhaps this was the answer?" She wrote a letter to her wayward son telling him to come home to marry the mother of the child who looked just like him.

The son obeyed. He married the farm girl when the child was four months old, even though he did not believe the child was his. The child was three years old before he recognized her resemblance to him.

The grandmother loved and cared for the child when no one else would. The grandmother often said there would never be another child like this girl no matter how many children her son and his wife had. There never was another child like her, she was a girl and the next three children were boys. The grandmother died when the child was barely eighteen months old.

The farm girl's dreams were again shattered. The young man didn't change as his mother had hoped and the young farm girl became more bitter and angry as time passed. The story did not end like Cinderella's, happily ever after.

The child grew feeling both uniquely special, lonely, unwanted, and blamed for her mother's unhappy state of affairs. She felt unsure of her place in the world. It must be said that she never heard the story of her birth until she was a grown woman even though the story shaped her and formed her life in deep and profound ways. Sometimes she still wonders who she would be if she had been adopted.

I had always known there was a story about my birth and I knew my parents had to get married. Dad told me that much when I was in my early twenties out of his fear that my mother's two older sisters would tell me in a mean or hurtful way.

When I was thirty I became interested in astrology and wanted to have my chart done. I was unable to get a copy of my birth certificate. Mom would not discuss the matter with me and at one time told me it was the worst thing that had ever happened to her. I am ashamed to say that the way I got her to open up to me was to get her drunk, but getting her drunk so she would talk about my birth did not work. I can really believe that from what I know of little North Dakota farm communities and of my mother's family my birth caused her great shame and humiliation. Certainly her family shamed her and humiliated her. Their own shame and humiliation caused them to have no sympathy or offer any support. They just wanted to get rid of her, all except her mother who found the Fred Finch Home in Fargo North Dakota, where I was born.

I took my father out to lunch and he shared that he had been contacted by the Bureau of Statistics to verify that he had married my mother in my lifetime. He explained, at the time of my birth, the policy was to write "BASTARD" across the birth certificate in big red letters. After my father had signed the affidavit in front of a notary, they sent me a certificate of birth but never the original certificate.

The Comstock Laws prohibited sending any obscene material through the mails, birth control literature was considered to be obscene. Many states banned the use of all birth control except by the most rudimentary methods; condoms, rhythm or withdrawal were the only options for birth control.

My mother had gotten pregnant the first time she had sex. My father, not believing he had fathered the baby, did go to Wyoming to work on an uncle's ranch. My grandmother, Ruth, did intervene and my parents did marry when I was four and a half months old. Dad told me that it was a common myth of the time that women could not get pregnant the first time they had sex. After I heard the story of the circumstances of my birth I decided to honor my grandmother, who saw to it that I had a home, by changing my name to "Ruth." Most of my family still calls me

Beverly even though everyone else has called me Ruth for over forty years.

Prior to deciding to change my name to Ruth I had talked about changing my name for over a year. Many of my friends thought it was such a good idea that they all had changed their names before I found an appropriate name for myself. One of my friends who changed her name did her master's thesis on women who change their names. I think this is the first time I became really aware of my influence on people. My ideas could change others.

My earliest memory as a child in North Dakota happened before I was a year old. I remember being in a crib and hearing my parents yell and scream at each other. Shortly after the birth of my brother, Elvin, we moved into my grandparents' house on a hill.

I don't remember my grandmother's death. She had a kidney removed about twenty-five years before my birth. She was given only five years to live. In those days she was a medical statistic because she far outlived her expected life span. Dad, however, remembers the trip to the hospital fifty miles away. He knew his mother was dying. She was turning black before his eyes and swelling up. She died of kidney failure in the Bismarck hospital. Three days after her death Dad claimed he had a vision of her reassuring him that she was all right. Even though I don't remember her death, I know losing her was one of the greatest losses of my life.

I believe it is her love and care that probably saved my life. Her death took all her love and care away from me. There was no one else who took her place or who understood the importance of loving and caring for a child in ways that were not just about food clothing and shelter. As I write this, I still experience the grief that is so associated with the loss of love and caring at such an early age

My childhood in North Dakota was mixed. My father's drinking became more of a problem. My mother's family had all left for California. Mom was not a person who knew how to relate to others and she was extremely dependent on her family for her sense of worth. Her little sense of worth and of belonging was shattered when she got pregnant with me. Mom wanted to please them and worked hard at pleasing them. I don't think she ever pleased them. So the fighting, the bitterness and hostility became more and more constant and more severe. Yet, I found solace in nature, in the setting sun, spring flowers, fleecy clouds, radio soap operas and of course in the Sears Catalog. Nature soothed my troubles and the Sears Catalog fed my elegant dreams.

Chapter 4

NORTH DAKOTA (1935–1937)

*She lay on the grassy hill, watching the prairie, seemingly endless.
Restless she began to look for Indian tea and paused again.
Looking at the little town down below, experiencing spring.
And she felt the warmth and smelled the earth,
Freshly turned, and she was excited — so excited*

The years in North Dakota, the first six years of my life, were frightening, confusing and unbelievably lonely. Even as a child I had a sense of never knowing what would be next. When my grandmother, Ruth, died I was eighteen months old and we moved to the house on the hill. It was what we might now call a bungalow. You entered the living room, went through a square arch into the dining room and then on the right side of the back wall, there was the swinging door to the kitchen. Off the living room was the front bedroom. Off the dining room on the wall by the living room was the middle bedroom. Next to the kitchen was a huge closet, which had once been a bathroom. Having the bathroom on the same floor as the kitchen was frowned upon. It was unsanitary. Off the same little alcove as the ex-bathroom, now closet, was the third bedroom. Behind the kitchen was big glassed-in porch. Located in the porch was the long flight of stairs to the basement. The toilet was now located down these stairs.

I shared the third bedroom in the winter when we needed a place for chickens so they would not freeze, and again in the spring when the chicks were hatched and needed to stay warm. During those times I moved into my brothers' bedroom. I also lost my space to the hired girl, a high school girl who worked for her room and board or to the latest teacher who boarded with us when she was teaching. I remember one of them; her name was Mary Ann. We called all teachers by their first names. At these times I slept in my brothers' room.

The times when I slept in the back bedroom I would have terrible dreams that frightened me. The one that was most frightening was an image of the coal bucket in the basement rattling when no one was in the basement. It was scary, I think because it was so weird. Another weird dream from my childhood that recurred for many years was the image of a person whose shape kept changing all night long, or so it seemed. The person would be fat and roly-poly and fill my vision and then it would change to tall and skinny, sometimes with a tall hat on his head. Sometimes it would be tall and long, sometimes it would be tiny and could be either skinny or fat. Sometimes all the space of my vision was filled with the fat roly-poly being. Both dreams frightened me and to this day I don't understand their meaning or if there was any.

In the kitchen there was a pump over a sink. Hot water was heated on the stove. There was an icebox, used only in the summer. The stove used coal or some kind of coal oil. In the floor was a trap door and under the kitchen was a cistern used to store water. The kitchen was the place for Saturday night baths in a huge round tin washtub. Everyone took a bath in the same water heated by adding a teakettle full of water after every bath. This was the house.

We had a generator that we used some for electricity, but mostly we used kerosene lamps for light. The generator was primarily used to power the washing machine on the glassed in porch. There was little else in the house that might have used electricity. The yard was just dirt and gravel, surrounded by fenced pastures. In one pasture was a bull and, in the other, two colts. Next to one pasture was the clothesline for hanging clothes. If I was warned once a day I was warned a dozen times a day to stay away from the pastures because the bull might break through the barbed-wire fence and gore me and the colts might jump the fence and trample me. Fear of something horrible happening fed my active imagination. Still to this day I can in my mind create truly horror stories about what might happen. Most of the time now I can dispel these stories. My biggest regret is that I did not know how to dispel them when I had a young family. I almost became my mother. I was so terrified of being like her. When I discovered any way I was like her, any mannerism I had that reminded me of her, I worked and worked to rid myself of it. I can remember diapering a child and holding my tongue on the side of my mouth between my teeth just like my mother. I was mortified and worked diligently to rid myself of this mannerism. Unfortunately, her anxiety, her fragile self-worth and my father's self-pity and guilty incrimination became the standard for the four of us as we grew from infants to young children.

Down the hill was a path next to another fenced field. That was the family garden. I remember it as big as a city block. In the spring and summer my Dad worked in the garden every night. The days were hot and humid and the thunder and lightning often filled the sky and the air with the smell of the storm, acrid and earthy. During the day, he worked in the WPA, the Works Project Administration, an ambitious New Deal program that employed mostly unskilled workers to build public works projects. Almost every city had a park, bridge, new roads, streets or building built under the WPA. In North Dakota one such project was the swimming pool located somewhere on the prairie close to Arena, maybe between Wing and Arena.

By the railroad tracks we had three other patches, a potato patch, a melon patch, a pumpkin and squash patch. Summer squash and winter squash and pumpkins grew together. I have no idea how we watered the garden. Water was such a precious commodity. We had rain barrels everywhere to catch water and a water tank built high above the ground. The tower was built to store rain and snow water and was probably used to water the gardens. Food was not a problem.

In the late summer after the chickens had been moved outside for a while, my mother would begin canning. She would kill chicken after chicken, wringing their necks as they protested with their loud squawking and then, headless, they ran frantically around the yard until they finally died. Thus came the saying, "like a chicken with its head cut off." I watched with a kind of curiosity that dampened my feelings of horror. Then she would pluck their feathers, singe them, cut up the chickens, and can them. She used a pressure cooker canner, so she could can raw chicken safely and save the extra step of cooking them and then canning them. They would cook in the canning jars. We also had fried chicken almost every night during the killing season. Then the harvest of vegetables began and she canned peas, string beans, carrots, corn and tomatoes. In North Dakota our vegetable bounty was limited by a short growing season, freezing winters and a serious lack of water. Usually we had an abundant supply of fast-growing foods, like head lettuce, some leaf lettuce, radishes, green onions and cucumbers. We did not grow things like kale, or spinach or chard, or broccoli. Fruit was limited to apples that arrived on freight trains, because apples kept well. During canning season, my mother's anxiety about botulism was contagious. It took me a long time to eat canned string beans because they were the worst culprits. Why? I don't know. More fearful than the bull or the colts or the rabid dogs or the thunder and lightning were the things I could not see: milk fever, botulism, rabies, tetanus or the many fatal diseases, which caused my mother's anxiety to rise. Twice I had a serious infection on my foot, one time from stepping on a rusty nail and the second time from a blister on my heel. I suppose when I reflect back on the "rusty nail" incident it was the most frightening, since I was reminded or the consequences of stepping on a rusty nail—tetanus, and death. Somehow I had escaped.

Oranges were rare and were usually a Christmas treat as were a variety of nuts. My father's favorite nuts were Brazil nuts, which were most commonly called "nigger toes." When we lived in California we were cautioned, warned and scolded into never again using the term, "nigger toes." As a child I really did not understand what this injunction was all about. There were so many injunctions and fears it just became another thing to worry about or be scared of making some horrible mistake. I learned to worry well and create story after story about the dangers in the world.

In the late summer the watermelons were harvested, as were cantaloupe, potatoes, beets, turnips, carrots, parsnips, rutabagas, onions and rhubarb. Beets were pickled, as were cucumbers. Potatoes, turnips, rutabagas, carrots and parsnips along with apples were readied for the icehouse and stored in the basement until the icehouse was filled with ice. Some were canned. Pumpkin and squash were both canned and what was not canned was stored in the icehouse. The rhubarb was used immediately for rhubarb pie or stewed rhubarb. I have never understood rhubarb strawberry pie. What a way to ruin a good rhubarb pie.

The only food we bought was flour, sugar, baking powder, and baking soda. Sometimes my parents would buy chocolate for baking or powdered cocoa for hot chocolate. Or my Dad would buy a huge hunk of chocolate for eating. We had eggs from the chickens, milk from the one cow and every year a hog was butchered. I watched my mother boil the milk to pasteurize it, always telling us a story about some child who died from milk fever. She even made her own cottage cheese. We ate well, and better than many of the families around us who did not own enough land to have a cow or a large enough vegetable gardens. I often heard of the family that lived on cornmeal porridge. In the morning it was porridge and then for lunch and dinner it was fried and served with syrup.

Every fall a hog was butchered for meat. It was considered my father's job. Unfortunately, my father was not very reliable. Between alcohol and gambling he might come home and he might not. I remember the time he did not come home and the hog was ready to be butchered. My mother was stuck with the job, which she did as she swore, mumbled under her breath, yelled and cried. I now understand how overwhelmed she must have been with four children in five years, an alcoholic husband, and her family thousands of miles away. In reflection I see her as a ship floundering in the North Dakota wheat, unskilled and scared beyond belief.

My mother yelled warning after warning at us. "Watch out for the dogs that wander into the yard! They might have rabies." Until I was in my sixties, if I went to someone's house, especially at night I would phone before going and ask them to keep their dogs in the house until after I had arrived. A barking dog was especially frightening to me. "Stay away from the pastures, you will be trampled or gored." "Don't let a cat near your face, they will suck all your breath and you will die." "Stop, don't pick that plant (chamomile) to make tea, it might be poison." In North Dakota it was called Indian tea. "Stay away from the railroad tracks, a train might be coming and you might be run over." "Get away from the window you might be struck by lightning!"

Another warning was of the gypsies who at times wandered over the countryside. When the gypsies came we were not allowed outside. They stole children and they might steal one of us. We were not the only children warned about the gypsies; every child in town was warned. If anyone saw any sign of a gypsy, the word spread like wildfire and children were hurried into their respective houses to hide in safety. To my knowledge not one child was ever stolen.

Lightning terrified my mother. There were always stories of new barns being burned to the ground by a lightning strike or the lone farmer on a hill plowing being struck by lightning before he could find a safe place. When a storm arrived we were immediately called in the house and warned not to go near the windows or anything in the house that was metal to avoid the shortwave radio and telephone. The only safe place was in the middle of a room.

My dad would load all the kids he could find and drive us to a swimming pool built by WPA workers and located somewhere on the prairie. My mother was terrified and even though every kid living in our little six-house town played in the pool, it was too scary for us since we had been warned and warned about the possibility of drowning. I never learned to swim.

Our fear was supported over and over by her fear that our father was going to die of puncture wounds from falling on the barbed-wire fence coming home drunk or be killed falling down the basement stairs on his way to the bathroom. There was always some horrible accident waiting to happen. If all this were not enough, every day there was some horror story. Everything was dangerous, nothing was safe, and we all grew up fearful and anxious, and we all lived it out over and over again all of our lives.

We also had a storm cellar under the house. It was there in case there were tornados or cyclones, or the most common name, "a twister." I remember a few times staying in the storm cellar waiting for the storm to pass.

I don't remember doing anything that met my mother's approval. She accused me of lying so many times, I could not tell when I told the truth and I began to question everything I did and everything I said. There was always something wrong with me. At least that is how I felt most of my childhood, if you could call it a childhood.

Chapter 5

THE NORTH DAKOTA YEARS
(1932–1937)

She found crocus growing in the melting snow.
First she was shocked and then delighted
To find a flower growing there.
Excitedly she ran to find her mother
To share her wonder.
But her mother seemed not to care.
Now I know where she has gone.
Silently inside, unwilling to come out,
Fearful of never being heard.

When I was less than five years old I loved to listen to soap operas on the radio. I listened to *Ma Perkins, Stella Dallas, Our Gal Sunday, Pepper Young's Family* and many more. It was a constant fight with the hired girls, who worked for room and board. These girls came from local farms and stayed in town so they could attend school. I believe the youngest might have been an eighth grader and the oldest a senior. They wanted to listen to country western music and I wanted to listen to the soap operas. I wanted to know how other people lived, and about other places.

There were ways my childhood in North Dakota was truly wonderful. I loved the plains and the ocean of grass. I loved the sunsets when the sun looked like a loaf of bread between two very low hills. I loved the daffodils on the hills, collecting Indian tea, making a lard bucket full, drinking it while hiding from my mother who was in fear of me accidentally poisoning myself. I loved the first crocus in the snow, the spring garden, and the first watermelon and summer rain. The mud, the cracked hard earth and the patterns made when the earth cracked fascinated me and fed my imagination. Maybe I could make dishes from these beautiful pieces of earth. I loved the sky and lay for hours creating my own scenes from fleecy white clouds. I also loved the birds that lived on the prairie. There were robins, nightingales, meadowlarks, hawks of all kinds, owls and the usual sparrows and swallows. I remember seeing birds on the fencepost, singing away and I loved listening to them. What was outside the house was my home.

I once learned a poem that I recited in a state contest and won second prize. I loved poetry. I loved the barns, collecting eggs in hay and the solitude. I found peace and solitude in the out of doors. I hid in the grass where no one could find me, where I could pretend I hadn't heard my mother's voice calling me. I suppose my greatest sadness from that time of my life was there was no one to share these meaningful pleasures. I was terribly lonely and felt like I did not belong. Yet all of this made life bearable for me and to this day I find great peace in nature, outside my home. The difference is my house feels like home as well as what surrounds it.

The parts of nature that were hard for me were animals. We had an old collie that was my uncle's before he left for California. I watched my Uncle Norval sob behind the barn on the day he, my grandparents, my Aunt Elma, and Aunt Ethel climbed in the car and drove down the road to California. All my mother's brothers had already left. I watched my youngest uncle sobbing as he waved goodbye to Fido through the back window. I also loved that collie. Before we left for California, my dad shot Fido. My mother was fearful of dogs, cats, thunder and lightning, horses and cows. All stray dogs were rabid and might bite, cats would suck our breath. Horses, cows or bulls might trample us. I never developed an affinity for these animals. I have more affinity for snakes, lizards, wild creatures, and especially for birds, than I do for domesticated animals. Farm animals had their place and their jobs. The dogs helped guard the property, or were used for herding or hunting. Cats lived in the barn and caught mice, rats and other small and unwelcome rodents. Animals did not live in the house.

Religion was not a part of my early life. Because of my mother's experiences with her father's family, she was antireligion. Besides, they were too busy with survival; there was little time for religious concerns. Somehow we learned some little prayer to recite at meals, if anyone remembered. I also learned to recite; "Now I lay myself down to sleep. I pray the Lord my soul to keep. If I should die before I wake, I pray the Lord my soul to take. God bless Mommy and God bless Daddy and make me a good girl. Amen." Reciting this prayer seemed more important than the meal prayer, but not important enough to be part of our daily rituals. Many things I now take for granted were not part of our ritual, brushing my teeth, washing my face and hands before bed. Washing my hands before meals or after going to the bathroom was a rare event. Baths occurred once a week, as did having our hair washed. Clean underwear or clothes on a daily basis never happened unless there was some kind of accident. Then it was a major issue. Clothes were washed on Monday, ironed on Tuesday and that included underwear, sheets, and towels, even bras.

All three of my brothers were born at home. I was the only child not born at home and was not breast-fed. Feeding babies by breast was a necessity in those isolated North Dakota towns. I remember when my last brother was born how we were all rushed out of the house down the hill to neighbors. A couple of the women stayed to help my mother give birth. After his birth the three of us were herded up the hill to see the new baby, but not touch or get too close. My mother was physically abusive to my brother, Elvin, and continually verbally abusive to me. She took out her frustration on my oldest brother and me. My two younger brothers escaped most of her wrath. Elvin often had appendicitis and needed to be rushed to the hospital some fifty miles away, which scared my mother. When she was frightened it quickly turned into anger. I think she simply blamed me for all of her misfortune; after all, wasn't I the reason she had to marry and end up in such an unhappy and miserable situation? Wasn't I the reason her family shunned her and abandoned her and left her to fend for herself? I most often felt hated by her and it is safe to say that I cannot remember any acts of love from her, except on occasion before she died. Even my children have commented on how cruel she was when she talked to me. I was so accustomed to it, I didn't even notice.

My brother Elvin was such a beautiful baby with his amber eyes and deep dimples. He was called "Baby Boy," until he was about two and half years old, if not older. Finally my grandfather put a sign around his neck, which read, "MY NAME IS ELVIN" in bold letters. Of my brothers he had the hardest time. He was the most abused by Mom and the most neglected by Dad. Before he was five, he had set the kitchen on fire when he lit a gunny sack to see if it would burn and the kitchen and the gunny sack both began to burn. The smell of smoke woke my mother from her nap. When she entered the kitchen her anger was hotter than the fire she extinguished. After she put out the fire, she beat Elvin so badly she broke the wooden coat hanger she was using.

My mother was hysterical at least once a week. It was in some way the nature of farm life in a barren country where everything was scary. My brother Charles disappeared one day. My mother's first thought was the gypsies had stolen him. No one had seen any gypsies around the countryside. The search began. Every outbuilding was searched, all the countryside was searched, the railroad tracks, the water tower. No sign of Charles. She became convinced he had fallen in the cistern under the kitchen and had drowned. Just as they were removing the lid located in the middle of the floor, there came a yell from one of the bedrooms, "Here he is, I have found him. He is under the bed asleep." As everyone rushed into the room, a man on his knees was pulling a shoe out from under the bed. There was a foot in the shoe that was attached to a body. My brother looked sleepily up at everyone, surprised by all the attention. It took my mother some time to calm down and relax. She was always on edge, tightly wound like a spring, just waiting for the next awful thing to happen.

My grandfather, Frank Lambert, took over the position of postmaster after my grandmother, Ruth, passed away. There was a case of penny candy in the post office. Each day we would go to the post office and get our one piece of candy. Our grandfather did not pay much attention to us so I for one often helped myself to more than one piece. If he knew, he never said a word about it. Finally he gave my mother a jar of pennies and we would take one penny and buy one piece of candy. Again I almost always took more than my one piece. He believed he could not provide us with free candy without providing free candy for all the other kids in town.

Frank Lambert was good to us in many ways. I am sure he helped my family financially. Once he gave me a beautiful wooden bench that I could use in playing house. He said it was my dining room table. My mother would not let me have it. "It was too good" for me to use in playing house. Another time he gave me a beautiful set of china dishes. I was very proud of them and careful with them. They were stored in a glass cupboard in the dining room. One day after much begging my mother allowed me to take them out of the cabinet. All three of my brothers were yelling that they wanted to see them also. I protested to my mother, "They are mine and they will break them."

She insisted I share with them. They stood in a line. I would hand a dish to Elvin who in turn handed it to Charles, who then handed it to Roy, my youngest brother, who then dropped it on the floor and broke it. My mother sat nearby sewing and never said a word. When I finally protested to her, she simply angrily said, "Why did you keep handing the dishes to them?" Stunned, I had no answer.

My mother was a beautiful creative seamstress. Her family that had moved to California frequently shipped a box of second-hand clothes to her. She would make my brothers suits out of someone's discarded suits and from the dresses that were sent, she made dresses for me. We would go to some little theater, or school gym somewhere and see a Shirley Temple movie. We would come home and she would find a dress in the pile sent from Oakland and copy a Shirley Temple dress for me. She was always disappointed; I did not resemble Shirley Temple. She tried hard to get my hair to curl by twisting it on rags and then she wound my hair around her finger again and again to make "Shirley Temple" curls. She would try the dress on me, pin it, take it in a little here, let it out, and shorten it only to lengthen it. She wanted everything just right, but what she could not get right was that I did not look anything like Shirley Temple, and in spite of her best efforts I was never going to look like Shirley Temple, sing like her or dance like her. I was a huge disappointment. Somehow I understand now why all of this was so important to her, but at the time I was just miserable. My not belonging was a reflection of her not belonging.

People were hard for me, especially the other children in this small town. They teased me, ran away from me, and I was always "it" when we played hide-n-seek or other such games. One time I cracked my wrist while playing tire tag. The tires were laid out flat in a row and you jumped or ran from tire to tire. You were safe only when you were on a tire, but could not stay on one tire for more than a few seconds. I was crying and in pain. The other kids laughed at me, called me names and never took seriously that I might have been really hurt. I went up the hill to my home, crying all the way. I don't know how my cracked wrist was diagnosed but I was told that it was not broken, just cracked.

One day in a barn behind one of the houses down the hill, two boys suggested I take off my panties and they would take off their underwear. I was probably five years old. I was hesitant and they said they would not be able to see anything through my dress, I think I did pull down my panties, but I don't think they pulled down their pants. I imagine this was not an uncommon event in communities all over the country and I suspect it may be less uncommon now, and certainly not considered quite as evil as it was when I was a child. There was one older girl who lived in Arena part time who would stand up for me and tell the other kids to leave me alone and not tease me all the time.

I was allowed to attend first grade when I was five. There was no kindergarten. The first eight grades were in one room on the first floor of the two-story brick schoolhouse. The second floor housed the high school. The teacher that year was staying with us and she thought I could handle the first grade. What I loved about school were the plays and the teeter-totter in the schoolyard. For the Easter play my mother made me a yellow crepe paper costume. I was a flower. For the Christmas play I had a blue crepe paper costume. I was an angel. The highlight of my school career in North Dakota was memorizing a poem and reciting it in Bismarck, in an auditorium on a big stage. Or at least it seemed big to me. I won second prize. I was so proud of myself. I had never felt so important. I knew someday I would show all these people who had been so mean to me.

The poem

The Moo Cow Moo
My papa held me up to the Moo Cow Moo
So close I could almost touch,
And I fed him a couple of times or so,
And I wasn't a fraidy-cat much.

But if my Papa goes in the house
And my mamma she goes in too,
I keep as quiet as a little mouse
For the Moo Cow Moo might Moo

The Moo Cow's tail is like a piece of rope
    All raveled out where it grows;
And it's just like feeling a piece of soap
    All over the Moo Cow's nose.

And the Moo Cow Moo has lots of fun
    Just switching his tail about,
But if he opens his mouth, why then I run,
    For that's where the Moo comes out.

The Moo Cow Moo has deer on his head,
    And his eyes stick out of their place,
And the nose of the Moo Cow Moo is spread
    All over the Moo Cow's face.

And his feet are nothing but fingernails,
    And his mamma don't keep them cut,
And he gives folks milk in water pails,
    When he don't keep his handles shut.

But if you or I pull his handles,
    Why the Moo Cow Moo says it hurts,
But the hired man sits down close by
    And squirts and squirts and squirts.
    (Bow—encourage clapping)

    North Dakota holidays were usually pretty simple. Since my mother's family lived in California, there were fewer people around. I don't remember if we had a Christmas tree or not.

Trees were pretty scarce in North Dakota. I do remember the red bells and garlands made out of red crepe paper and I remember I believed in Santa Claus. After moving to California I looked for the familiar Christmas decorations that I knew in North Dakota, but never found them. Now on occasion I see red crepe paper bells and garlands. One year relatives from all over sent me a doll for Christmas and of course my parents got me a doll also. I ended up with twenty-eight dolls. My mother was beside herself. I know I did not keep all of them. I could not understand why she was so upset. I know I threw a fit and got to keep three of them, but it was a battle.

On Easter we had Easter eggs and often I remember those little yellow marshmallow chicks that were truly awful. We lived up the hill and these holidays were not celebrated with the other children in town, except for the Easter play and the Christmas play. The only holiday shared with the local townspeople was the Fourth of July. Dad would get fireworks and as soon as it got dark all the other families would head up the hill to our house where Dad provided a real fireworks show. It was very exciting and I felt important since we were the only family in town who had a fireworks show. On the Fourth of July there was always something like a carnival, with rides, games and even airplane rides. Mom's father loved to ride an airplane. As important as these holidays seemed, Farmer's Day seemed much bigger with a Ferris wheel, a merry-go-round, airplane rides and air show, booths, even a sideshow. We were not allowed to attend the sideshow. These carnival-like events did not happen in Arena, but somewhere else in a field close to Wing. There were always a lot of treats at these carnivals and one was pop—orange and vanilla, which I loved. Like everything else all the holidays were colored by fear. Would my father come home or not? Would he be drunk or sober? The likelihood was he would be drunk or surely on his way. If he was not falling down drunk, he might convince my mother to join him and that almost always led to a fight, if not physical violence, a lot of yelling and screaming, until someone ran out of steam and went to bed. Their dance colored my life until I left home. It also flattened my life force and almost squashed it.

This is what I remember of the North Dakota years. As I was writing this I began to wonder, "Did I really win a prize for reciting a poem?" Or was it just my fantasy to fill my own holes, to believe someday I would be wanted, loved and important. "Did my mother actually make little suits for my brothers?" Or had I looked at too many Sears Roebuck catalogs and saw how little boys dressed in other parts of the world. My picture of the world outside of Arena was informed by the soap operas on the radio and by both Montgomery Ward and Sears Roebuck catalogs. I remember when you could buy a house from the Sears Roebuck catalog. When the catalog arrived twice a year, I was hooked. I spent hours looking at everything and planning my "grown-up life." I loved the catalogs and waited each spring and fall for their arrival. I think it is a safe assumption on my part that my picture of the world was very distorted. In reflecting back I believe everyone's images of what life "should be" was distorted by catalogs, the distant radio and finally motion pictures. I was sure if I could look like the girls in the Sears Roebuck Catalog, then I could be one of the women on a soap opera and then I would be loved. I searched and searched for what it was, one had to do to be loved. I knew that in movies people were loved and in the soap operas also. I knew they looked more like the people in the Sears Catalog than I did. So maybe if I looked like those girls in the catalog, I might be loved too.

Frank Lambert died of cancer. The cancer had started on his nose and it spread until finally he died. I remember the day of his funeral. My mother was wearing a black dress, a black hat. The dress had a square neck with white lace. I felt her anxiety about how my father was handling the situation. I watched her standing by the back door wondering if he would come home and get her to go to the funeral and whether or not he would be sober, slightly drunk or falling-down drunk. I was so curious, but I knew I was not going to this event; it was not for children, was the constant refrain I heard when I asked about it. My father did get home in time to take her to the funeral. We did not have memorial services in those days.

The next thing I remember is loading up the new Ford V8 my father had bought with the money from the sale of the house. He was so proud of this new car. I cried as I watched him taking Fido behind the barn to shoot the old dog. I thought of my young uncle crying behind the barn some years before as he piled into another such car to go to "The Golden Land," leaving Fido behind. I was in awe, watching a truck pull a huge flatbed, carrying our house down the hill, our home disappearing, moving to a new location. I never forgot the house. Much later in my fifties, I learned it had burned down and still I felt the sadness of the loss of home.

I remember the people coming up the hill, either walking or driving beat-up old cars to shake hands with my father and saying goodbye. My mother sat tight-lipped in the front seat of the car. Some of these people promised they would see us when they too went to California and some of them did. Others just shook their heads and proclaimed my father was always a little on the wild side and this proved how crazy he could be. It never occurred to one person that my mother had any say in this decision or that it could have possibly been her idea. Many people were just plain sad to see us go, and still wished my father "luck." Finally we drove down the hill and out of sight of the little town where I had spent the first six years of my life. I visited North Dakota fifty plus years later and did not recognize one thing except my great-grandparents' farm and my grandmother's family home. I have never wanted to return and I have thought often of the people who share their longing to return to the place of their birth, of their childhood. I have never had that desire. The Bay Area became my home.

Chapter 6

THE TRIP
(1937–1938)

Once there was a child sitting on the porch after a scorching day.
Eating the first summer watermelon, tasting the sweetness,
The juices running down her chin.
The sun descending between two prairie hills, like a golden loaf of bread.
And she asked herself, "Where did it go?"

I don't remember much about the trip. I remember the back seat was fitted with a piece of plywood extending the seat to make room for four children. The back seat had no foot space, just one plank with blankets and pillows. Under the plywood was storage for a variety of unremembered items. I remember my mother's fear as we drove over the Rockies and my father's fear not far behind. My mother had never seen or been near a mountain. Mom had never been more than fifty miles from the farmlands surrounding Wing and Arena, North Dakota, except when she went to Fargo to have her first child, me.

I don't remember if we slept in the car or stayed in motels. I think we often slept in the car, but on occasion stayed in a motel. I suspect that there might have been times when we kids slept in a car and my parent slept in the motel. The trip was slow. It was the biggest adventure my parents had ever had. Both of them were frightened. My mother's fear was centered on the narrow roads, and the elevation. She could not help herself as she looked out the window at the steep fall into some canyon. During the trip the look of fear replaced every other facial expression she had, except maybe anger. Her fantasy about California and family kept her determined and on the road, while inside she was filled with terror. She never had misgivings about the purpose of the trip, "a new life and being reunited with her family." My father's fear was centered on the hazard of pulling the small, but heavy trailer behind his new car. The trailer carried all of our worldly belongings. We left behind all the books my grandfather owned and I loved. I loved the collection of books by Alexandre Dumas, the short stories by O Henry and the many other books on the shelves that were left behind. I don't know when if ever I forgave my mother for leaving the books. I begged to take the blue crystal fruit bowl with matching candlesticks. There was no room for anything that was unnecessary. My father was on the trip, leaving his beloved North Dakota for one reason, his hope it might make my mother happy.

We drove through the Badlands and my parents were so awestruck that I was also. We drove through Sioux Indian land and the stories scared me. We looked up at the faces carved in Mt. Rushmore and I was inspired. One face was not quite done. I don't remember which one. All the faces were completed by October 1941.

No one in the car had been farther than fifty miles from where they were born with the exception of my father, who had traveled to Alaska as a baby with his mother to join his father, but it was too late, his father had already found another woman. He returned to Whitehorse, Alaska, at the age of eight to visit his father and his new wife and meet his half sisters. He went to Wyoming to avoid marrying my mother. And here he was married to her with four children. The daughter he denied and three sons. He often seemed puzzled as to how all of this had happened to him as well as puzzled about being on this trip to the "Golden Land." California.

I don't know how long the trip took, but I suspect it took at least five to seven days. It was a hard slow drive. The draw of the "Golden Land" and her family kept my mother focused. We must have asked at least a dozen times a day. "Is this California?" "Is this the Golden Land?" "Are we there yet?"

I don't remember the route we took, but I do remember the mountains. I remember vaguely that at some point we were in Oregon. As we got closer to California the excitement in the car was palpable. Everyone was excited, except my youngest brother, Roy who was barely three. He was just tired and cross.

Finally my mother announced as we passed a sign proclaiming we had entered California, "We are here! This is California, this is the Golden Land!!" I don't know what I expected, but it was not more of the same. The same highway we had been driving for what seemed forever, the houses looked the same, the landscape had not changed one bit since we had left the Rocky Mountains. I was shockingly disappointed. I think I even expressed my disappointment, wondering what was golden about it.

I think I began to feel the power of California when we drove across the Golden Gate Bridge and then the newest wonder of the world the Bay Bridge, barely finished. Both bridges were new and of course the talk of everyone everywhere. We arrived on Colby Street in Oakland to be greeted by most of my mother's family. As I reflect back, it was quite an experience for all of my family. My brothers, my parents, and I saw things we had never seen before. We had never seen a refrigerator, a gas cooking stove, sidewalks, an indoor bathroom, and a faucet with both hot and cold water, a streetcar, and a modern grocery store. I remember the Safeway Store some blocks away. I believe there is still a Safeway on that particular site. I ate my full share of chocolate-dipped ice cream cones from that store. The ice cream bars in my grandfather's bar were not nearly as intriguing as the sugar cones with ice cream dipped in chocolate. I was hooked for many years on Safeway's chocolate dipped ice cream cones.

I had never seen a building of more than two stories and of course the buildings I am referring to were two-story houses. The old brick schoolhouse had two stories and that was about it. A building more than two stories high was a wonder. The grain elevators were the only structures more than two stories high on the North Dakota landscape. They marked the location of the railroad tracks, a train station and the little town of Arena. They stood alone in the middle of the prairie next to the railroad, tall sentinels overlooking the bare flat land.

When I think about it I could go on and on about what was new: milk in a bottle, bread in a wrapper, peaches, avocados, artichokes, apricots, plums, and even purple plum trees lining the street. Roller skates and bicycles were a wonder to me. It was a new world except the chaos was still there.

We all lived with my grandparents in a basement apartment. This was not a large apartment so it was very crowded. When I think about who lived in the apartment, I know my grandparents were there, as well as my Uncle Norval, my Aunt Elma and probably my Uncle Ervin. Then you add six more people and you probably have eleven people living in a two-bedroom apartment. My Uncle Harold may have lived there at times also. My mother's oldest sister, Ethel, had recently married and had moved to her own apartment with her new husband. The brother just younger than my mother, Leslie, was married and had a baby. He, his wife and child also lived in an apartment. My Aunt Florence was not living in the Bay Area at that time. I remember someone putting two armchairs together to make a bed for one of us kids. I think that was my bed. I imagine my brother Roy slept with my parents and my brothers Elvin and Charles slept on each end of the couch. I felt suffocated, cramped and sometimes overwhelmed by the pressure of so many people in such a small space. Apartment buildings were also one of the wonders of California.

All the adult males in my family would report to the Carpenters Union each morning in the hopes of getting work. At night almost everyone drank and there were always bickering and fights, as well as laughter, teasing, making fun of others and criticism. The food we ate did not change much. We ate very simple North Dakota food, meat, potatoes and vegetables. My grandmother would take the streetcar to the store and buy the cheapest cuts of meat. She would cook one pound of beef short ribs in a lot of water, throw in a lot of vegetables and more salt and pepper. It was a little more interesting than "stone soup" but not much. It was called beef stew. We sometimes had a salad made from iceberg lettuce. My Aunt Ethel worked also. The chaos would swell and shrink but it never disappeared. I learned quite young if I helped I could get by. I helped! I watched babies and younger children. Often the children I watched were less than two years younger than I was. I was five or six when we arrived at Colby Street. Often Claudia, Uncle Leslie's baby, was left at the house and I took care of her as well as my brothers. I changed diapers, folded clothes, peeled vegetables, set the table and cleared the table. Sometimes I would dry dishes.

I was teased mercilessly. I did not understand much of what was happening. A well-known tactic was for the grownups to speak in Finn, the official name for the language is Finnish, but that was a term rarely used in my family. More often they spoke some mixture of Finnish and English, having conversations assuming that we kids could not understand. Usually I could piece the conversations together or at least I thought I could. How well I did I will never know. I never mentioned what I heard. Most of the conversations were judgments, criticism and gossip about whoever was not present. Ethel or Florence, when she was visiting, usually led these conversations. My mother was often one of their targets as was Nettie, Uncle Leslie's wife. Sometimes the conversation would be between my grandmother and grandfather. The men in the family also used a combination of Finnish and English to share stories about their so-called sexual conquests and their negative opinions or a kind of black sexual humor. The men's conversations were much more lively and humorous than the women's or so it seemed, since they all laughed and laughed. I picked up more of their conversations since they could not speak Finnish as well as the women in the family. I heard more dirty jokes by the time I was eight than I have ever heard since. The exception was my Uncle Ervin who spoke Finnish as well as the women. It seemed he never quite belonged anywhere in the family. He spoke excellent Finnish, played the piano, and sang. If he had any sexual conquests I don't remember hearing about them.

The house where the apartment was located was an old brown shingle, two-story house so common in the Bay Area. The owners of the house were Mr. and Mrs. Hammer. An old bamboo desk that Mrs. Hammer gave to me resided in my grandparents' house until my grandmother died, now it belongs to Char, my oldest daughter. It was a family neighborhood and there were kids who did not know the "North Dakota story" and who taught me about roller skates, hopscotch, how to play jacks and ride a bike. I loved jacks and hopscotch best of all. I was both curious and fearful. Everything was so unfamiliar and so new and I knew making a mistake could be terrible. In my home, children did not make mistakes. I had been "slow" in learning to tie my shoes. It was a long time before my mother got over being so humiliated by having such a stupid child.

A woman who lived up the street took an interest in all four of us and was kind to us. It was the first time I was around children and we just played together and had fun. No one teased me, or made fun of me or called me strange names. Then a strange thing began to happen. Large sheets of butcher paper began to appear in the backyard with dire warnings on them. I don't remember the warnings. I know that all the kids in the neighborhood including my brothers and me were both scared and excited. It was a mystery. The mystery was never solved. It could have been older kids, or it could have been one or more of my uncles or it could have been the real monster, the one we all looked for around the corner, in the garage, in the basements of the neighbors. The hunt kept us busy until we left Colby Street.

Our stay at Colby Street was short-lived. The old conflicts between my mother and her sister Ethel began to flare and the men's drinking got more frequent and worse. My father loved it. Rarely was any one of the men sober on the weekend. Even Aunt Ethel's new husband joined in the barhopping and drinking. Sometimes the women would go along. A favorite activity was to go to a sauna on Friday night and then to a bar. I think it was during this time my Uncle Leslie's wife left him and took their child and moved to live with her family in Washington. None of us ever saw his ex-wife or child again. His daughter's name was Claudia. When someone in the family tried to contact her long after she had grown into a young woman, she would have nothing to do with them.

We left, packed up our trailer again and moved to Port Orford, Oregon, where Grandfather Grover, more commonly known as "Slim," lived with the mother of his last child, a girl named Sandra who was slightly older than my youngest brother. We called her Aunt Sandra and were puzzled to have an aunt younger than ourselves. Ollie and Slim lived together in a small house near town. My father got a job at the local lumber mill and we lived in company housing. A person who somehow became important in our life was a man named Axel who lived in a house on the millpond, or a small lake or maybe a river. I remember how often the house flooded. He seemed particularly fond of Ollie and Sandra. Later the story we heard was that he was Sandra's real dad. Finally, one time when she visited us she told us she was sure Axel was her real dad. Yet when Grover died and was buried in Red Bluff she came to the funeral. My dad was the only real family she had with the exception of a distant cousin who owned the restaurant in Port Orford. After Grover abandoned this, his third family, Ollie and Axel did get together or so the story went.

No matter where we lived it was never a place that one would call "golden." My mother tried and wanted desperately what she never had and so we were always on the lookout for the "golden" place where things would magically became better. As for me, I still looked in the Sears Catalog and I had begun to make paper dolls. The catalog became my "golden land."

Chapter 7

PORT ORFORD, OREGON
(1939–1940)

The sky began to roll and darken.
And there it was, rumbling and bright,
The cracking sky!
She felt the first drop, the second, the third,
The rumbling grew loud, the cracking bright, oftener.
And the water fell and fell. She heard her Mother's call.
Quietly she waited and did not answer.

I had seen the ocean. I am sure my mother, who planned our route, made sure that we went past the ocean or at least over the Golden Gate Bridge. She may have heard about the ocean in letters from her family in California, but to see the ocean must have been a huge thrill for this very bright young woman who grew up on a farm and never lived anywhere but in a farm town. We all entered a world none of us could have imagined. But the ocean in Port Orford was special. We could walk on the beach, sit and watch it crash against the rocks. But most important of all, we could tempt it by walking in the shallows until the tide turned and we ran as fast as was possible, so we would not get wet or, in our young minds, drown. The ocean was a wonder to me as were the sand and the huge rocks and the shells that were like nothing any of us had ever seen. The color seemed unreal in the intensity of the blue or the deep green. The sun setting over the ocean was one of the most beautiful, magical, spectacular sights I had ever seen. I looked for that sight everywhere I lived or went for most of my life. I still consider it beautiful, with all the different shapes forming and reforming. I loved nature more and more. Waves, capped with white and bigger than my father, caught my breath. But the solitude and calm I found in the clay, way back on the beach, close to the trees, is beyond words. I loved this place and was overcome by the beauty of it. It became my sanctuary. Every day I would go to the beach after school and lie about it to my parents. I stayed after school to "help the teacher" more than any child anyone remembered. I had again found my home, on the beach and in the forest surrounding the little lumber town.

But daily life in Port Orford was hard and frightening, especially for my mother. She had her first "real" job, cleaning crabs in a crab factory, another new experience for her. Dad worked in the mill and he now had his long-lost father to encourage him in his gambling and drinking. This is the first time he had seen his father since he made the trip to Alaska as an eight-year-old. There was no real family support. My mother's family was still in California and the only real support the family had in North Dakota, my step-grandfather, Frank Lambert, was dead. All the ways my parents had understood life were gone. There was no hired girl to help my mother with her four children, or to help with house cleaning or cooking, washing clothes or doing the ironing. She was still living with her alcoholic husband and trying to keep food on the table, often not very successfully.

The small house had only two bedrooms. My parents had one and the four of us slept sideways in one bed. There was no place for a garden. Farm animals did not exist. Food was scarce. Sometimes we had nothing but bread and milk. On occasion we did not even have bread or milk. We were often hungry. The school provided us with a cup of soup for lunch and some days that was our only substantial meal.

It was here I experimented with cooking. I was seven years old and decided to make cookies. I almost knew the recipe by heart for sugar cookies and I could read well enough to figure out the directions in the cookbook. I did not have a measuring cup, or measuring spoons. That equipment did not become part of my household until long after I was married. There was sugar, butter, flour and an egg. I could not find vanilla, but I did find vinegar. In my mind they were probably the same since they started with the same letter. I did not have cookie dough; I had something like cake batter. I baked it until a toothpick stuck in the middle came out clean. When my mother came home, I cut it and we both tasted it. It wasn't bad, but it certainly did not taste like any cookie I had ever eaten. When I told my mother about using vinegar in place of vanilla, she just laughed. If I remember correctly, my brothers and I ate the "cookie cake." After all, food was food and at that time any food was better than no food.

Ollie's cousins, who owned the one and only restaurant in town, realized how grim the situation was and hired me to babysit their young son in the restaurant while they worked. I was seven years old, already skilled as a baby sitter. The child seemed totally out of control, racing through the restaurant, playing in the flour bin and generally making one mess after another. I worked for food. One time, my mother recalled many years after we left Port Orford, there was no food, none! No milk, no flour, nothing. She was beside herself trying to figure out what to do, when a neighbor she worked with in the crab factory knocked on the door and invited us to a crab dinner. He had been crabbing and caught quite a few and he knew none of us had ever tasted crab. My mother jumped at the chance. I still smile to myself when I think of this hungry family being saved by a crab feast.

Between work and the Pastime Saloon my father was rarely around unless a bunch of families got together to party. Grandfather, Slim, dealt poker at the Pastime and it was the family hangout. I grew up in saloons. The first was Grandfather Josephson's saloon in Wing, North Dakota, and then the Pastime in Port Orford. Saloons were like second homes to me. So much of our life revolved around time spent hanging out in saloons. Later, it was the neighborhood bar in Oakland, the Til Two, where my uncles and dad hung out and it became a familiar place for me also. I was going to the Til Two with some family member until I was at least eighteen. I could not drink liquor, but I could drink cokes.

Saturday nights were party nights. After the Pastime closed everyone would adjourn to someone's home to drink, play cards, drink, dance, and drink and drink some more. On one of these Saturday nights the party was at our house. Finally sometime in the late evening the four of us children went to bed and fell asleep. In the morning when we climbed out of bed the house was a disaster—cigarette butts every where, half-empty glasses, some with cigarette butts floating, along with half-empty bottles of booze, beer and mixes for the booze. My brothers decided to do what the adults did and began to drink what ever they could find. My brother Charles was the ringleader and he drank more than either of my other two brothers. Roy, probably the least amount, being the youngest and Elvin, my oldest brother, almost immediately began throwing up. By the time my parents crawled out of bed all three of them were sick and Charles the sickest of them all. After much screaming, blaming, accusations and phone calls it was determined that Charles had alcohol poisoning and, at least according to my mother, he almost died. My mother stayed home, but my father could not miss a baseball game. Everyone assumed she was just overreacting. My brothers had good teachers on drinking, horseplay and irresponsible behavior; my dad, and my mother's four brothers all contributed to their education. The role of women in the family was to work and take care of the men. I also had my role—work hard, cook and clean, take care of the kids, make sure the men were happy. Even in my house as a child the boys were the favorites.

Sunday afternoons were baseball games. The legend was that Slim had played briefly first base for the San Francisco Seals. The legend was probably started since Slim was lean and tall. The adult men in town would play baseball against some other team from another small town. It really was just another excuse to drink, mostly beer.

We often heard stories about Peeping Toms and about other unsavory characters that hung out around town. One night I was staying all night at Ollie's. Sandra and I were sleeping on the couch. We had not fallen asleep, when Ollie called to me to come to the bedroom and she told Sandra to stay where she was. We were both just kids, but Sandra was younger than I was by about three years. I walked into the bedroom and Ollie immediately shushed me and I crawled into bed by the wall with the window. Ollie then said in a loud voice, "Beverly, hand me the gun in the corner." She pointed to the window and there was a man pressed against it trying to spy on us. The window was covered by just one of those flimsy pull-down window shades.

Shaking I responded, "Where?" The man moved slightly to the side of the window.

"Shh! There isn't one, just pretend there is."

Again shaking, "Here," as I pretended to hand her a rifle.

Very quickly she told me to grab a coat and get Sandra and follow her to the car. The three of us ran to the car and we jumped in as fast as we could, I, wearing my underwear and one of Slim's coats, Sandra, her mother's jacket, and Ollie was in her nightgown and her own jacket. We arrived at the Pastime where Slim was dealing. All three of us were terrified. Ollie was hysterical. Slim, cool, calm, kept on dealing. I don't remember if anyone did anything or if the incident was just set aside as "part of life."

I remember Port Orford by the events that occurred there and I also remember it by the environment. I, to this day, think of it with fondness. Why? I really don't understand. Most of the events were just plain terrifying. But the landscape was different from anything I had seen before and it was strikingly beautiful, intense and wild.

The company house was in a community of such houses, simple and basic. No yards or gardens, just a house on a gravel street. Across this street lived this very strange woman, who either befriended my mother or mother befriended her. My mother seemed to need one friend, whom she could always complain about and find fault with. The neighbor woman had a collection of dolls that she literally treated like children. She talked to them, changed their clothes, and generally treated them as if they were human. She often came to our house in the evening and stayed late into the night. On one such night, my brother Elvin had left his school reading book at her house. When it was time to leave I was to accompany Elvin with her to get the book. As we entered the house and she opened a closet to hang her coat, a voice from the closet said, "Hello." The woman began to scream and yell at us to run. She started running and Elvin followed her and I froze on the spot where I was standing. Elvin turned around and grabbed me, pulling me out of the house. Dazed, I too began to run. As we watched from our house we noticed that each light was turned on in the house, room by room, until the house was ablaze with light. Sometimes we could see this hunched-over figure move across the house to the side door, the door to the kitchen.

Shortly afterwards we heard the woman's brother had been released from prison. Perhaps it was he who scared us all so badly. I don't think anyone really knew. He hung around the neighborhood and was clever with his hands. There was not much he could not build. My brothers were allowed to hang out with him, but I wasn't. My mother was a skillful predictor of dire events, which to my knowledge rarely came true. One of the things he constructed was a trapeze bar about eight feet off the ground. It was in a tree and there was a ladder and some kind of platform so we could reach it. Since I could not play with him or the boys I worked out on this trapeze bar to learn tricks. I think I was trying what was called "Dead Man Fall." It required swinging from your knees and getting enough momentum to do a flip in the air. I did, but landed on my tailbone rather than my feet. I knew I had hurt something, and I had learned a long time ago not to tell anyone when I got hurt. I didn't tell anyone, but I continued to bleed from the rectum for about a week. To this day

I do not know what I might have injured, if anything. I became more anxious than I already was.

The school was a nightmare for both Elvin and me. Charles may have started school in Port Orford but Roy was still too young to attend school. I remember Elvin was in first grade when he simply had his foot out in the aisle. I certainly have never thought of it as deliberate, but the teacher who tripped over it did. She broke a ruler beating him for this infraction. Elvin was the subject of most of my mother's violent outbursts from the wooden coat hanger she broke when he burned a gunnysack in the kitchen in North Dakota to the times in Port Orford where she would kick him as punishment for kicking someone.

I was in the second grade and I was supposed to know how to read, but more important how to "sound out" a word. I could read, sort of, but I could not sound out a word or figure it out from the sounds. I could not spell and that holds true for me today. In the second grade I cheated on the spelling tests and of course was caught and "made an example of" by the teacher. I was humiliated, not only was I dumb, but I was also bad. Worse, both my brother and I were bad. We came from a bad family. It was a major relief for me to read an article somewhere that the research on spelling indicated the ability to spell was not a skill one could learn. You were able to spell or you weren't. Further, this ability had nothing to do with intellect. True or not, I chose to believe this piece of research. I was so relieved.

There were wonderful times also. There was this secret cove off Highway One between Port Orford and Gold Beach where we went on picnics, and could go across the highway to play on the beach. There were shells and beautiful rocks on the beach to collect. After school I would sneak down to the beach to play in the clay and make pots and other wonderful items. A small lake that we had to row across to visit friends provided me with a sense of adventure. Unfortunately, that was quite rare since my mother was so sure the boat would tip over and we would all drown. Huge, beautiful flowers and all kinds of wild berries, most of them edible, filled the forest. Berries and huge, beautiful flowers were a new and wonderful experience for me. Also in the forest was an abandoned half-finished house. It was my dream house. I rebuilt the house in my mind over and over, I furnished it and made it beautiful, or at least I thought it was beautiful. I did not want to share it with anyone, ever.

Probably what scared me most and deepened my sense of responsibility for the well-being of the family was the evening my father found me down at the beach and came to take me home. I knew something was terribly wrong. I had thought, as a seven-year-old child might, they believed me when I lied about staying after school. My dad was more sober than I can ever remember him being, more serious and quiet. We drove home in silence. The only thing he said to me was, "Your mother needs you." We arrived home and went into the tiny house and my mother began to scream. She was covered with bruises. Her face and her arms were covered with huge black-and-blue bruises. My dad said little. He simply left. I was shocked and terrified, and yet I knew I needed to pull myself together. If I did not, the consequences would be more terrible than they already were. I think my brothers stayed overnight at someone else's house.

I cried and I remember crying every day for a long time. The next day my mother went to see an attorney and swore over and over again, "He is not coming back. He is never coming back." At the time it seemed to be directed at me and I suppose it was since many years later she told me, "The only reason I took him back is because you cried so much." My mother's "never" might last about one week. Over the years, my mother swore over and over again, "He is never coming back" so many times I think all four of us lost track of how many times they separated. We packed up and again headed back to California. This time my mother had a plan. Her plan involved buying a house. Where they hoped to get the money is totally beyond me.

Chapter 8

WHEELER STREET, OAKLAND, CALIFORNIA (1939–1943)

Kicking the dust with her toe, she felt the warm dryness
Of the dirt on her feet, on bottom.
She felt the moist coolness as she patted
And shaped the wet mud.
Oh they were beautiful these pies—her very own creations.
She left them to bake in the hot sun, smug, satisfied.

Wheeler Street was part of my life until I left the Bay Area, it was never called anything but Wheeler Street. When we lived there, it was Wheeler Street, not the house on Wheeler Street. We lived many other places and when we visited grandparents, aunts, or uncles it was still just Wheeler Street. When I talk to my two remaining brothers we still refer to it as "Wheeler Street."

How to describe life at Wheeler Street is a real challenge. It was a rowdy, alcoholic, barroom kind of place. It was a place of religious fanatics, filled with sin, hell and brimstone and occasionally redemption, whatever that meant. During the war it was an open house to anyone passing through from North Dakota, South Dakota, Minnesota or any place else in the middle northern United States. For a child it was often frightening, since drunkenness was dangerous and so was the violence, but it was fun sometimes and exciting. For the young girl, Beverly, the attention from men did not feel safe and sometimes it was not. It was a man's house dominated by male energy, male needs, male games, such as stud poker, five-card draw and another ten or twenty men's games. It was loud. Both men and women were loud. It was a house of backbiting, teasing, faultfinding, blame and often deception. The house lacked maturity, love, kindness and the manners and behavior of most of the homes that surrounded it. It was as if the house was dropped there from some other wild and woolly place. Nothing about it fit or was consistent. It was unreliable, unstable and sometimes dangerous.

Somehow my mother had found a way to buy the two-story house in Oakland, on the corner of Wheeler Street and Fairview. I suspect her oldest brother Ervin loaned her the money, on the condition that their parents could live there. The street was one short block long, and a long block off Shattuck Avenue. The house sat on a very small lot, not much bigger than the house. The front yard was tiny and the back yard not much bigger. The neighborhood was made up of similar houses and on the far corner there were a few stucco houses. In the middle of the block was a very small rundown house.

It was a mixed neighborhood of old people and families. In the house next door lived two older women. They taught me how to gather lavender and make sachets to sell door-to-door in the neighborhood. It was my first experience with lavender. My first customers were those two women. In a house on the corner of Wheeler Street and 65th Street lived a tailor and his family. He had one son and they were Jewish. Next to them was an Italian family with an older girl who had already left home and twins, a boy and a girl. I remember every Saturday morning they scrubbed the kitchen floor on their hands and knees and then waxed the floor. The house was spotless and the front part of the house was never used. The family made it clear, with the drawn window shades and the somber attitude of the inhabitants, that no one was welcome. I had been in the house rarely; when I went over, we played in the basement. On Saturdays I would wait for the girl twin, Darlene, on the back porch landing.

On 65th Street were two families with children that I knew. One was a boy named Matthew, much older who seemed to be exceptionally bright. This family's last name was Marshall. I think there was also a girl who was much older. The basement was Matthew's. It was a large space with low ceilings and exposed rafters. It was a perfect place for an electric train, scientific experiments and electrical devices totally unfamiliar to me then and now. He had an elaborate electric train, and loved electricity so he had all kinds of things he had made and wired. There was a Morse code key, a telephone, a radio that he had build and rebuilt. I thought the place was magical. I could hardly imagine one person having all that room. It was a room that no one entered without permission, a room that even his parents never visited. It was his space, his room. I was so impressed that he could make and run all the things in the basement. It was his territory and no one ever bothered him there. I longed for a space that was just mine, something I had never had and could barely imagine.

Across the street was another house with children younger than me. The girl's name was Carole and her brother was too young to play or go to school. I was again fascinated by how the family lived. The mother would be vacuuming the house every morning, her hair combed and styled, wearing a dress that was not at all like the house dresses my mother and her sisters wore. She wore pumps and nylons. In my book she was the kind of mother I wanted and was never going to have. She was elegant with beautiful black hair and always had on her makeup. She was the "Hollywood mom."

In the rundown house in the middle of the block lived one boy. I think he was a year older than me. When he invited me to the movie and I went up the street to ask if it was OK, I might as well have announced that I was going to have sex. I was at the most ten and he was maybe eleven. My mother and her sister were in an uproar. Of course the answer was, "Absolutely not!" What was the matter with me that I would even have to ask such an outlandish question? I should have known better and why did he ask me? What were we doing, and from now on I was told to stay away from him. As you can see, nothing was ever simple.

Our house itself was a big house. There was a front porch, not huge, but a comfortable size to hang out on and play. The front door opened into a large entryway. Located on one wall were big wooden doors that slid open into pockets in the wall making the entrance the size of a double door. Across from the living room doors the staircase to the upstairs began. The stairs were wide and there was a landing before you climbed the last stairs to the upstairs hall, which was dark and gloomy. At the end of the stairs was a door that closed off the entire upstairs of the house. At the end of the entry way was the door to the everyday dining room, which opened to the kitchen. The back door to the house opened on to a small screened back porch.

Upstairs was my grandparents' apartment with its own entrance off the hallway. Also located off the hallway were two bedrooms and a bathroom. The bedrooms were always filled with uncles and cousins—always rowdy, always teasing me and telling tales of their "many conquests." Their conquests always involved women and sex. All of these men were exceptionally bright, talented and psychological messes. Everyone was a carpenter of some kind, or a handyman, or a day laborer.

My grandparents' apartment was large and comfortable. It had a door that opened from the living room to a long flight of stairs that led down to the sidewalk. It was one bedroom, a large living room, and a kitchen combined with a dining area.

Everyone in the house worked except Olivia, my grandmother, who like most Finns, was stoic, stingy, and unavailable. She and Elmer, my grandfather, had a good time together arguing politics and complaining about the state of the world. All my Finnish relatives had large families so I am assuming they had good times in some other ways, but there was never a hint of the relationship being more than a good discussion. Olivia was a diabetic and every morning she or Elmer would see that she got her insulin shot.

It was never clear to me who lived in the two upstairs bedrooms. I think Elma, my mother's youngest sister, had one of the upstairs bedrooms. Eventually I think she got an apartment closer to UC Berkeley. The other bedroom was where two of my uncles, Norval, the youngest, and Ervin, the oldest, slept at least until Norval went into the Army. Other people came and went. Where they slept is a mystery to me. It was always changing. Eventually, Aunt Ethel and her new husband, Jack Williams, a black Irishman from Boston, permanently moved into one of the bedrooms. They lived in that bedroom until we moved from the house. Jack never talked about his life before moving to California. If anyone asked he would squirm and change the subject. He was intriguing since he was "the mystery man." Jack was also kind, loved all four of us kids and was good to us and to my mother. When money or food was tight Jack would show up with a bag of groceries. He was an alcoholic. He and my youngest brother Roy were so close that I think when he died it was one of the major losses in Roy's life. It was rare that anyone wanted to be close to us or have a relationship with any of us. We were rarely noticed unless it served someone's need to have a scapegoat to tease, humiliate or just to make up jokes about. I understand how much Jack Williams meant to my younger brother, Roy.

We lived on the first floor of the house. There was a large kitchen, two large dining rooms, which was a good thing. The house became the center of all holiday celebrations for the next ten years. During WWII any time a soldier passed through the Bay Area, my grandfather would have a big traditional holiday dinner. Since the holiday dinners, Christmas, Thanksgiving and Easter were always the same, the fourth, or fifth or sixth dinner was just like them.

I think my parents had the bedroom in the back of the house and the four of us had the parlor for our bedroom. I believe the second dining room would have been what was then called the living room, but was used as a dining room. Living in that house for the one or two years was the highlight of my mother's life. Many years later, there was another time that came closer to the life she had once imagined for herself. When the family lived in Red Bluff and we four had left home, she was able to create the home she had always wanted, even though the house was a simple tract home among many other tract homes in Red Bluff. They remodeled it and she bought all new furniture and her first sets of crystal, china and sterling silver.

All four of us attended Peralta School. None of the other kids in the neighborhood attended school with us, except Bobby, the boy in the rundown house who had invited me to a movie. The twins on the corner, the girl and boy who lived on 65th Street with the "Hollywood mother," all attended the Catholic school across the street from Peralta School. The Jewish boy and the Marshall boy were all enough older that they went to a different school.

Peralta School was then and would be today an exceptional school. Art, music, dance, and literature were as important as math, reading and writing. The school had a difficult time placing us. I think I was first placed in Miss Harry's third-grade class. The teachers at Peralta School believed we were probably behind the children at our appropriate grade level and placed us one grade lower to make sure could keep up with the other children. We were all quick learners. After about two weeks I was moved to Miss Smith's fourth-grade class and both my brothers were also advanced one grade. It was a new experience for all of us. Since leaving North Dakota, it was the first time we had a relationship with a teacher where we were treated with kindness and respect. In North Dakota we often gave room and board to the teacher for the school year, while she taught in the old brick two-room schoolhouse. Her status in our house meant we were treated well by her. The first time any of us had been treated in a school as if we might be intelligent was at Peralta School. I think my school experience at Peralta School greatly influenced how I wanted to teach when many years later I became a teacher.

There was one African American boy in the school. He was in first grade when my brother Charles entered the class. Clarence was asked to show my brother where to put his lunch in the cloakroom. My brother followed Clarence into the cloakroom. Clarence asked him for his lunch. My brother, standing as far away from Clarence as possible, stretched out his arm with his lunch bag in his hand; when Clarence reached for it, Charles quickly pulled his arm back. None of us had ever seen a Negro before. It was quite an adventure for all three of us. As we lived in the neighborhood and might drive across Adeline, we would enter the neighborhood, which was almost entirely made up of an African American population. From then on, we had many experiences with blacks, especially when we moved to Richmond. At the time I was growing up in the Bay Area there were different acceptable terms for African Americans. Among them were Negroes, "blacks" and "colored people" or "colored folks," depending upon one's own regional or ethnic origin.

We were probably the poorest family in the area, even poorer than those who lived in the rundown house across street. We were poor not because no one had jobs or could find work. We were poor because of my father's alcoholic gambling behavior. Unfortunately he had a lot of company and cronies for his behavior, my mother's two brothers and Jack, Ethel's husband. We could afford only one pair of new shoes a month. I can assure you they were not very expensive shoes. By the time my turn for new shoes rolled around, there was not much of a sole left on my shoes. Cardboard would be cut every day and fit into the bottom as replacements for the soles. Someone's shoes would be totally without a sole before it was their turn and we all would be pushed back a month. My shoes lasted a little bit longer than Charles' and Elvin's. Roy's shoes lasted about as long as mine did. Charles and Elvin often got two pairs of shoes to our one. Shoes were a very big deal in my family and were one of the major expenses. The rest of our clothes were purchased in thrift stores, which totally embarrassed my mother and me. If my mother had not been so embarrassed I probably would not have been at all. The two other sources for clothes were hand-me-downs from one of the rich houses where Aunt Ethel worked and from Peralta School. When one of the teachers asked any of us if we knew what size we wore, I began to recognize that meant we would be getting clothes. Somehow a bag of clothes would make its way to our house. I suspect that the teachers noticed when we looked particularly shabby. I think the whole situation embarrassed and deeply humiliated my mother. All of these experiences contributed to my mother's feelings of inadequacy. My mother had no time for sewing, especially not for the elaborate tailoring she did in North Dakota.

Chapter 9

WHEELER STREET AND LIFE OUTSIDE
(1941–1944)

She helped her Dad milk the one old cow
Tasting the warm bubbling milk on her fingers.
The barn smelled old musty and damp.
The sky looked black,
She stopped, watched, heard the rumbling roar
As her dad walked in the house carrying the pail of fresh milk
And she followed behind.

When I first started at Peralta School I dressed quite differently than the other girls. They often made fun of my clothes, especially my white but very dirty majorette boots. I suppose in an effort to get really sturdy shoes for me, my mother had probably found them on sale somewhere. When they were no longer fit to wear and I was wearing just ordinary oxfords, one of the girls in my class asked me what had happened to my boots and I told her they had worn out. She then asked where I had got them and of course I did not have a clue. About two weeks later she showed up at school wearing white majorette boots and soon they were the rage in the fourth and fifth grade.

    I never felt quite like I belonged. In the fourth grade when we would draw I was teased about my drawings. I worked hard and learned how to draw and eventually became quite good at it. When we sang, the kids in class laughed at my funny voice. I am not sure my brothers were doing any better than I was.

Miss Geary, my fifth-grade teacher, changed my life. She always greeted each child every morning. After we were settled she would make comments about how well our clothes looked, how the colors matched or how the pleats hung so evenly. I can tell you, I worked overtime to dress so that she would notice me. It was a very big deal to be noticed by anyone who was kind and respectful. Every day she made a point of noticing who we were. We also took turns arranging flowers. The classroom always had a bouquet of flowers and someone would be assigned the task of arranging them. After they were arranged Miss Geary would comment on the arrangement. She taught me about beauty. The school had its own library and a gymnasium. Someone would come to the school a couple times a week and teach physical education. Someone else would teach singing and playing an instrument, which I now know was a recorder. We wrote poetry. It was a new world for me. It opened a world I never knew existed.

It was that year I really learned to read. I was in the fifth grade and probably could read in some fashion, but in the fifth grade I really learned to read and love it. I read everything I could find. I would carry a stack of books home from the school library and then from the public library. I read every possible book in the school library and the public library. In the public library they would not let me take out adult books. I tried on occasion, but I was always stopped. I could not tell you all the books I read. I remember reading *Little Women* and then moving on to all the other books by Louisa May Alcott. I think I read because it was a place to escape, it was a way I finally learned about another world that existed, but was not my world. It was so much more than my world. Books soon replaced the Sears Catalog as my source of information about how other people lived and what the world was like outside of Wheeler Street.

Another way Miss Geary helped me was to keep me after school and she would play a note on the piano and then I would try to match it. By the time I was in the fifth grade I had a very high shrill voice. I was so anxious. With Miss Geary's help I learned to modulate my voice and talk more normally. I don't know of anyone who was more of an influence on me as a child than Miss Geary. It was as if I existed for the very first time in my life. I was truly seen. Peralta School and Miss Geary began the change of my life. I began to get a glimmer of how other families lived and what it meant to have some social skills and a sense of how to dress. I wanted to fit into the group, be part of something that I never even knew existed. I don't think even I recognized the change; I just knew I was different than I had been. I read all the time and became interested in the larger world, a world I had never even thought about until the fifth grade at Peralta School. It was not the world I took for granted or just knew, like most of the kids that surrounded me in Peralta School. It was during this time I convinced my mother to give me piano lessons. The teacher came to our house and the lessons were very short-lived. The teacher informed my mother, it was a waste of his time and her money. I was devoid of musical talent. My efforts at learning to tap dance met with the same fate.

While living on Wheeler Street all of us four kids came down with the mumps at the same time. While still living in North Dakota, I had whooping cough and diphtheria almost at the same time. It was the first time I had been really sick. My mother who had been a sickly child had not had the mumps. It was not long before there were five of us down with the mumps. Staying in bed was quite important, especially for the boys since you did not want the mumps to go "down on them," that is, cause swelling and pain in the testicles. It was also important for adults to stay in bed and, if I remember correctly, in dark rooms. How true any of this was, really? I don't know. There were so many myths and beliefs, true and false, that swirled in my young head and all around me that may have been based on fact and may have been based on empty space. I never knew which was which. My Mother had to stay in bed as she was swollen down to her breasts. Aunt Ethel, my mother's eldest sister took care of all of us. One day she announced, "I have changed my name and if you need anything you will have to figure out what my new name is." None of us ever figured out what her new name was. I suspect it was nonexistent. It was her way of handling the pressure of four grumpy sick children and her equally grumpy and miserably sick sister. Taking care of five people with mumps was a lot of work and, of course, the four children were very demanding and someone needed something most of the time. She also worked either at the Baldwins' family home or in a laundry. As the mumps began to disappear and we all felt better, we were more than a handful: we were an armful.

Our life on Wheeler Street was dominated by alcohol. No one was fond of movies or any life out of the family. Everyone worked. At night all the men would stop at a bar to have a few drinks before coming home. On weekends sometimes they would take me with them. I cannot even begin to describe how humiliating these times were. Usually at some time in the afternoon or evening one of them would turn to me and say, "Beverly, sing us a song. " I usually declined many times until finally one of them would say, "Look I will give you a nickel if you will sing us a song." In those days a nickel was a lot of money for a girl between the ages of eight and twelve. Besides, it was either sing or be badgered and badgered until I did, even if it took many drinking hours. I would sing something. It could have been anything from "The Old Rugged Cross" to "A Slow Boat to China." Everyone in the bar would begin to laugh and look at me. My uncle would hold out the nickel just out of my reach until I finished the song.

If I ever had any self-esteem it was pretty shattered by the judgments and teasing. "You have the Heaton mouth!" my mother would announce in disdain. Or another mother comment, " You are built just like your dad's half sister, Betty Leach, tall (over six feet) long legs and a short waist." Actually what I had was a short torso and very long legs. "You will never find clothes to fit." She never directly called me stupid, but there was nothing I could do "good enough," from sweeping the floor to washing a dish. It was her opinion and very soon mine that if you could not do something right the first time, don't bother because you aren't talented enough to learn. She never really taught me to do anything. She just complained about how I did everything.

My uncles' teasing covered everything else. They teased me about boys, and how I probably would never have a boyfriend. I looked too much like Eleanor Roosevelt, who was the homeliest woman in the world. They teased me about my protruding teeth and the worst was when I started to get serious poison oak. I then got the nickname, "itchy pants." I wanted to hide and in many ways I did. Mostly I became a caretaker and I did get some accolades for that.

In the summer I would help a woman named Elsie who had four or five kids and was someone's cousin, probably on my grandfather's side. I would spend part of the summer there, and then I would go to another cousin's house located in Sharp Park down the coast from San Francisco. Lillian Parchuck had heart disease and in the summer I would help her. Her husband, Matt, was a dour man who barely noticed my existence.

If no one needed my help then I took care of my three brothers, and we ate peanut butter and jelly sandwiches and drank root beer floats every single day. I had no way of controlling them or getting them to behave. I was ten or eleven years old, unskilled at managing three boys who had watched their uncles scapegoat me and make fun of me since they were little guys. They often followed their elders' example. I was frustrated, and so angry I was unable to contain my rage. I would yell and scream at them and when that did not work then I just beat them. Every day I would beat the hell out of at least one of them.

One summer, my mother's sister, Florence, invited me to stay with her and Art, her husband. They lived in Los Gatos. I thought with relief and hope, " There are no children for me to baby sit and no one is sick. I get to do what I want." I loafed and made paper dolls all day and every day for about six days. My paper dolls had the most complete wardrobes you can possibly imagine. They had swimming suits, shorts, skirts, blouses, evening gowns, hats, gloves and on and on. They had seven of everything, a multitude of different complete outfits for every single day. They had special outfits for any and every event, from Christmas to the Fourth of July. Then my aunt sent me home because I did nothing but sit around and was of no help whatsoever. She complained bitterly to my mother about my ungrateful behavior. I learned that if I wanted anything I had better work hard to earn it. I think I believed that most of my life and sometimes still do. It was a lesson for me. No one wanted me unless I worked hard, so I worked hard.

The men at Wheeler Street who stayed and who came and went frightened me and I kept up my guard with them. I was always fearful, nervous and uncomfortable around them. There were my mother's four brothers, Ervin, Harold, Leslie and Norval who came and went. One of them was always living in the house. Sometimes more than one of them would share a bedroom. Oscar and Henry Banttari filled in the gaps and lived in the house if there was room. A man named Amos lived there sometimes, as did another man who was much older. When he ate, he ate with his mouth open and sometimes food ran down his chin. I thought he was pretty disgusting, especially when I was helping at Wheeler Street one summer and he caught me off guard in the kitchen and grabbed for my crotch. If that was not hard enough, often one of the uncles or cousins would pull me on their lap and begin to hug and kiss me, it did not matter who was around, and joke about it with each other. One day as I fought to escape from Oscar's lap he said, "Come on what's the matter with you, I am just playing around." Lots of the uncles and cousins were around and as I escaped I announced, "I don't like it." Everyone thought it was all terribly funny.

It was not enough that I put up with all of these men, my Uncle Norval had a friend, Morris, who was always proposing to me and proclaiming to everyone his intention to marry me. I considered him extremely unattractive and besides I might have been twelve or thirteen at the time. I was a pretty angry kid and I took it out on my brothers whom I was responsible for, since I was their babysitter. My underground opinion of men was pretty distorted and weird and I believed deeply and profoundly I would never be loved, used, yes, but loved, no. There was no evidence anywhere to the contrary.

One of the most disgusting stories was when two of these men would go on a double date with women they had probably picked up at some bar and were still trying to get into the sack. They would go to a motel and get two rooms. The four of them would sit around and drink and maybe dance. I really don't know. Then one couple would go the room next door and both couples would go to their respective beds and fuck. I cannot think of a more appropriate word. When the women would finally fall asleep, one of the men would knock on the thin wall and they would have a conversation about the women in bed next to them, snickering and laughing. I was both curious about how that worked and shocked that the women put up with their behavior.

One of my favorite stories was about my Uncle Leslie who had a date with a rich woman. She drove a big new Cadillac. He was quite excited about the date and talked about how he would come home a "hero." Unfortunately, it did not turn out quite like Leslie thought it would. They drove to the beach in San Francisco and found a place to park. I guess it was pretty hot and heavy and they were both naked, when the woman stopped all the action and said she heard a noise and told Leslie to go check it out. It was clear nothing was going to happen unless he did. He got out of the car and began looking around and when he was checking the back of the car, off it sped and his clothes were in a heap in the sand or at least most of them were. These stories brought laughter and teasing. This story for me was about what all of these guys deserved. Somewhere along the line they all got married, except for Ervin, but none of them stayed married. Norval my youngest uncle did stay married. He was not much of a participant in all this. He was too young.

As I was writing this, an old incident that I had forgotten came quietly into my brain. I debated about whether to include it or not. It is terribly embarrassing and shameful. And yet I have such a strong commitment to truth telling I cannot leave it out. I am sure many kids could share this story. I began to hang out with the little Italian girl on the corner. She was close to my age, probably just a little younger than me. We spent time in her basement and I spent time convincing her to slowly undress as I watched and then to torture her with a willow stick, or to have her bend over and it probably would have gone on and on except she was never a willing participant. Actually, very quickly she refused and I gave up.

What is important about this story? I will never know where this game originated. Was I myself sexually molested? I don't know. Was I acting out all the stories that surrounded me and I heard from uncles and cousins? Or is it just the nature of what children learn when trying to make sense of the things they overhear from their parents' bedroom or from the adult conversations when they eavesdrop? Many of the therapists I have worked with over the years expressed a suspicion that I might have been molested. Once in my forties I asked my Dad if he had ever sexually molested me. His response, "I don't know, I was drunk and blacked out too much of the time." I still don't remember. I believe if I ever do remember, it will be time to grieve, to weep and work through the story, to clear and heal that place in my psyche.

Wheeler Street holidays were madhouse. You never knew who would come, or how many to expect. During the Second World War my grandfather would invite everyone. One of his nephews, a McCluskey boy, was on his way to the Pacific and he wanted us to plan a big family dinner for the young man. After that anytime anyone came through California for any reason, we had a holiday dinner. The dinners were always the same and any deviation was met with stern disapproval. There could be anywhere from twelve to thirty people attending. The menu never changed nor did who did what part of the dinner; there could be as many as six holiday dinners in a year, if not more. The turkey and ham were my Aunt Ethel's job. Vegetables, potatoes and Jell-O salad were my Aunt Elma's and my grandmother's job. Mom made the gravy and the pies. I helped by mashing the potatoes, doing what all the others asked, and I always set either one or two tables, depending on how many were attending. Both tables were full of turkey, cranberry sauce, dressing and gravy. Then there was ham, sweet potatoes, green beans, homemade bread and of course Jell-O salad. For desert there was pumpkin, apple, and mince pie all with a dollop of whipped cream. By the time I was sixteen, I began to wonder what would happen if someone changed the menu?

Hilda, one of Granddad Elmer's sisters, was often invited and sometimes attended. Sometimes her four children attended. They never seemed to fit in with the rest of the crowd. They were all quiet people and deeply religious. They did not fit in with the drinking, gambling and raucous conversation upstairs.

Great-aunt Hilda and Grandmother stayed downstairs. All the men went upstairs where the liquor and beer were. No one drank wine. They played poker, laughed, played music, told jokes, mostly dirty, and told their stories. Sometimes one of them would bring his current girlfriend. Then there might be some dancing. A favorite dance was the polka. The women who cooked and cleaned and got everything ready would take frequent breaks and run upstairs to have a drink or dance or play poker or listen to jokes. The upstairs was fun and the downstairs was about hard work. To protect his sister, Hilda, Grandfather had strict rules about what behavior was OK downstairs. Certainly none of the upstairs behavior was acceptable.

Now Hilda was as different from her brother's family as she could possibly be. She worked and I mean she worked. Her husband died leaving her with four small children and Hilda raised them, cleaned other people's houses and kept her own house immaculate. Her hair was pulled tightly back into a small bun. She wore housedresses and on Sundays and holidays a slightly nicer black or navy blue dress. The style was always the same. Buttons down the front, the length almost to the ankles, and always below the knee. She wore sturdy oxfords that had a slight heel. She never wore jewelry or makeup of any kind. And she was religious. She did not believe in anything but hard work. She did not believe in music of any kind, art, movies, dance, or games of any sort. She did believe in singing hymns. She did not believe in doctors, dentists or eye doctors. She wore glasses and would state, "They were the work of the devil and I had tried to break them by throwing them on the rocks, but was overcome."

Her children were all good people, somewhat more relaxed than their mother. Hilda knew how to pray and attend church. When dinner was ready and everyone came downstairs and took their place at the table my grandfather would ask, his voice slurred with liquor. "Hilda, will you say the grace?" Hilda said the grace endlessly and none of us were spared. She prayed and prayed for our souls. She prayed for us to give up our evil ways, to quit smoking, drinking and fornicating. She begged God to intervene in our sinful lives and get us to go to church to learn the error of our ways and to repent, repent, and repent. She asked God to save us from our sins and show us the way to heaven. When she finished dinner was cold.

Hilda died in her daughter Ruth's house where she had lived for several years. After spending some years in bed pulled into the fetal position and unable to make any contact with others, she finally died at about the age of ninety-six. Some of my relatives who are still in North Dakota still follow the same rigid religious beliefs.

Sometimes after dinner Uncle Ervin and Aunt Ethel would play hymns on the piano and sing. They always played "The Old Rugged Cross" and the other one I still remember was my grandmother's favorite and also mine, "In the Garden."

It was at Wheeler Street during a holiday dinner that my dad announced he had quit drinking for perhaps the tenth time in his life. Only this time it stuck and he never drank again. It was again at Wheeler Street that I remembered waiting for my dad to come home and take us for a ride. I would wait on the front porch while he ran to the store for a carton of cigarettes or beer or whatever he announced he needed. I waited and waited until there was absolutely no doubt and it was abundantly clear he was not going to be there to take us for a drive, and in fact he might not come home at all. Wheeler Street had everything, family, God and the Devil.

Chapter 10

THE WAR
(1941–1945)

She wandered over the cracked hard dirt, crossed the railroad tracks.
She gazed at her Dad's melon patch and wondered if she dared
She did!!
And was gleeful with her success.
Full and satisfied with her day, she lay in the tall grass and slept.
I wonder, where is that lonely girl now?

It was at Wheeler Street we learned about Pearl Harbor. The war changed our life almost as much as leaving North Dakota had. It was a time when everyone was gathered at Wheeler Street and we heard the cry of newspaper boys up and down the streets. "Pearl Harbor Attacked." We rushed out of the house to see the headlines as big as the front page. Shock lined the streets and filled the houses. I was nine years old when Pearl Harbor was bombed.

Everyone turned on the radio to listen to the news of this event and the announcement that war had been declared. The men soon left for the "Til Two," the closest bar. Along with the women and my brothers, I hovered over the radio listening.

Soon the talk was about air raids. In school we made mats of oilcloth stuffed with newspaper and stitched together to lie on under our desks in case of a bomb attack. We listened for the air-raid sirens and, not knowing whether it was a test or the real thing, we would hastily crawl under our desks and crouch down on our mats.

We hung blackout curtains in every room of the house. There were block air-raid wardens who patrolled the streets when there was a practice air raid. My grandmother never could obey the rules about the blackout curtains and often there would be a knock on the door to tell us to close our curtains or that light was leaking out the edge and to fix it. My grandmother would swear in Finnish. Her favorite swear word was "baaskka." I have no way to know how to spell it but this is how it sounded. It meant, "Shit."

Shortly after the air raid practices were in place we begin to hear about the rationing. Food was rationed; sugar, dairy products, meat, and more, margarine replaced butter on our table. I was often assigned the task of coloring the margarine. It came in a box in a single large brick and it was white. Included in the box was a little packet of orange coloring. An imitation cheese began to appear in the grocery stores. Some foods totally disappeared and the rise of imitation foods seems like the forerunner for all our processed foods, fast foods that fill the markets today. This North Dakota family knew how to skimp and they did. My grandmother would go to the market and buy a pound of short ribs to make stew for anywhere from six to ten people. Hunger was not new for any of us since leaving North Dakota. I remember a box of peaches in the downstairs kitchen in the Wheeler Street house and I ate the box of green peaches until I got sick. It took me a long time to eat peaches again. People started Victory Gardens and grew their own food. We did not. The lot at Wheeler Street was way too small and there was not much interest.

There was no wool for winter clothes, nylon stockings begin to appear to replace silk. Even cotton was flimsy and not very substantial. Women begin to work in places they had never imagined working before. They worked in the shipyards on the assembly line and they began to wear pants and kerchiefs to cover their hair. Shoes were made from synthetic material, and rubber soles and heels disappeared. Plastic products also begin to show up in the shelves. High heels became less and less popular. Makeup began to be harder to find. Women often wore only lipstick and no longer applied foundation, powder, rouge or eye makeup. Elastic for all practical purposes disappeared. Underwear had a button on the side with a buttonhole. Metal fasteners disappeared. Plastic replaced almost everything; even zippers were made out of plastic. Nothing worked very well. Once I was carrying a bag of groceries home when the button broke on my underwear and I barely made it home with my pants still on my body. They were around my upper legs. Old safety pins became the staple fastener. You could not buy them but we had plenty lying around our house to hold something in place until it could be fixed.

There was much you could not buy. Furniture of any quality, bedding, mattresses, towels, some clothes had totally disappeared. Tires were made with a synthetic rubber, cars were not available, and most vehicles were driven longer than they ever had been. Parts were hard to find for autos, refrigerators, and appliances. Fortunately, there was not nearly the amount of necessary tools to cook in the kitchen as we have today. Blenders, electric mixers, electric coffee pots, and the list is endless, had not even been invented yet.

Television was not available. The news appeared in newsreels at local theaters. Propaganda was at a new level and was being studied as to how to use it more effectively. Social psychologists explored how to make the most impact. For example, plant one story on the front page of the newspaper and hide the real story somewhere in the back pages. Another tactic was to publish a big story and then another one and another one and the first most important story would be forgotten. I think the art of fooling the public was in the process of being fine-tuned and it is even more effective now. I learned about all of this at a conference put on by the Golden Gate Group Therapy Institution in the Bay Area. The speaker had worked as a propaganda expert for the government.

We remained at Wheeler Street for another year and a half after the war began. I watched three of my mother's brothers be drafted. Leslie, Harold and Norval all served in the Army. Ervin, the oldest, got a deferment to stay home and take care of his parents. My mother once said shortly after the war that her brothers and fifty cousins had served in the military. I believe this was true. Remember, my grandfather was one of twelve children and one of his siblings had sixteen children and the rest were not far behind. What was important was the fact that everyone came home safely and then one of her cousins was killed in an auto wreck after surviving the war.

It was during this time I began to cook and clean on a regular basis. I had always cooked and cleaned, but now it was something every day. Added to these responsibilities was taking care of my brothers. In my mind my survival depended on being useful and needed. If I was not, the threat of being sold to the Salvation Army or given away to some stranger on the other end of the phone, might not be some joke, it might be real. One of my uncles or cousins or someone, but always a man, would get on the phone and pretend they had contacted the Salvation Army and would ask them, "We have a girl here and we just don't need her or want her, how much would you give us for her?" Or the conversation might sound like this: "We heard you needed a girl and we have one we will give you free." Did they tease my brothers in this way? I really don't remember. Sometimes they would include how useless I was and what a burden I was. I thought it was a joke, but I could never really be sure. If it was a joke, it was not at all funny, it was mean and cruel, but then I did not know what a horrible thing that was to do to a child. I do now and I know the price one pays.

I had been scapegoated so much of my life I did not know there was anything else. The scapegoating began first by my mother, then the children in the little town, and then by her family. My father seemed like a ghost in those years, and he was. Often he was in the shadows or would disappear completely in alcohol or gambling or both. My mother and her family were overpowering and seemingly sucked up all the air. When we became too much for my mother and she complained enough, my father would take the four of us into the front living room and begin his long lecture. The lecture could last as long as two hours. It began first with how badly we were treating our mother. How she did not deserve such treatment and then it would go into a long discussion about how wonderful she was. How grateful we should all be that we had her. Last but not least would be his overriding guilt about how he had failed her, failed us and in general what a schmuck he was. All through the lecture he would be sobbing in guilt and self-pity. I don't know anything I hated more than those horribly torturous lectures, I would rather have been beaten. A beating would last about two and a half minutes and then be over! The lectures seemed endless.

    As for me I lied and I lied well, primarily because I did not know when I told the truth and when I didn't. By the age of three I had been accused of lying about everything from misplacing my mother's scissors to hiding something or making up a story about the hired girl. I had gotten very deceitful and secretive. I acted as if I was alone in the world and had to make all the decisions about my life, and above all figure out how to take care of myself and never get caught. I was also incredibly absent-minded. I had created my own world and when I escaped into that world, I was apt to put a pair of socks in the refrigerator and the butter in the oven. I did not mind being absent-minded; everyone laughed and enjoyed my being forgetful and besides any attention was better than none and usually I got none. If I really wanted something I would never ask for myself, I would set up one of my brothers to ask for it. I would never ask to go to a movie or with someone in the car. I would get a brother to ask. It was most probably my brother Elvin. I was the number one scapegoat and he was number two. It would have helped him if my father had liked kids. He did not. It appeared to me, he disliked Elvin as much as my mother hated me. It did not help that he was named after Dad.

Finally, we moved from Wheeler Street at the end of the fifth grade or at the beginning of the sixth grade. My father's drinking was totally out of control and money was tight. It did not help that Ethel and her husband were now permanent residents in the bedroom upstairs. Again my mother hoped the move would mean she had finally found the "Golden Land." Maybe it was all of these things that initiated the move to Rollingwood, a low-income community located in San Pablo. Maybe by now it boiled down not to the "Golden Land" but the fear that none of us including her might survive.

Chapter 11

ROLLINGWOOD, CALIFORNIA
(1943–1945)

Screaming wildly, she swings down from the hayloft
On an old heavy rope.
She lands in the hay laughing until none is left.
Quick now, listening to the creaking rafters,
Wondering what is next.

Rollingwood was a suburban neighborhood located between Richmond and San Pablo. It was built to provide housing for the low-income population. It was different from the projects since the projects provided apartments and duplexes for rent and were managed by the Housing Authority. The houses in Rollingwood were for sale. It was one of the first efforts to provide affordable homes to the huge influx of families that came to Richmond to work in the shipyards. At that time it was segregated housing built exclusively for the caucasian population. It is hard to imagine Richmond, a small city of 23,000 mostly white families, almost overnight becoming a bustling multiracial city of over 100,000. The small city was unprepared for the new population and their needs, not only for housing, but schools, childcare, and medical facilities. Nothing was enough. Even harder were the psychological issues. The new residents were unfamiliar, seemed strange and often dangerous to prewar Richmond. The African American population had grown tenfold, Mexicans and Chinese populations had grown to such an extent they were visible everywhere, no longer just confined to their small section of the city. The city had been a mix of large rural areas, with animals, gardens and open space and a contained downtown of two or three blocks of city streets, some manufacturing, and the offices and refinery of Standard Oil. Near Standard Oil was a large indoor city swimming pool, the Richmond Plunge. All of this changed and changed rapidly. The adjustments for both the old and new residents were huge, tense, confusing and often frightening. Richmond was a new city, a different city than it had ever been or would ever be again. New tensions arose, mostly racial tensions; some of these tensions were directed by the old residents and some were between the new minority populations.

In Rollingwood the homes all had three bedrooms and one bath. There were not any sidewalks, but there were curbs and houses lining the streets in neat and orderly rows. The houses were situated at the foot of hills, golden in the summer and brilliant green in the winter. We had a small three-bedroom house and I had my own room for the first time in my life. My brothers shared a bedroom. Housing projects and low-income housing were still segregated. Rollingwood did not last long. We stayed maybe two years, but in my family that was about the average. It was the first time since leaving North Dakota that we did not live with family or less than a block away from them.

I don't remember much about the house. What I do recall is that I was getting to be a weirder and weirder kid. Even as I say this, Rollingwood offered me something I had never had before. It was closer to normal. Or how I had imagined normal. Even on Wheeler Street there was not another family where everyone lived together, aunts, uncles and grandparents. We now lived in an ordinary house. There was only one family in the house, but much was the same. My father still drank and gambled and might not come home on a Friday night until Sunday evening. My parents still had horrible fights and my mother threatened to leave on a regular basis. We were still poor; we still spent a lot of time on Wheeler Street.

By the time I was twelve I was cooking dinner more than once a week, sometimes as much as five times a week. Either my father or I did the laundry. My mother did the rest. Every night after dinner a battle would ensue about doing the dishes. When I cooked, it was my opinion I should not have to do the dishes also. My brothers' opinion was, of course, I should do the dishes, cooking dinner was no excuse, besides it was all women's work. Finally someone, and I believe it was my father, since he loved to organize things, came up with a schedule. If I cooked, I did not have to do dishes, when I did not cook then I would be part of the rotation, set and clear the table or wash the dishes, and the last job, dry the dishes and then all of us clean up the kitchen. This last job was a joke. We just fought over it and it never really got done. By that time my parents were so tired of it all, they ignored the condition of the kitchen when one of us announced, " It is all done." And we went to our rooms. Eventually, they finished cleaning the kitchen after we were in bed or it just stayed a mess until the next meal.

When I was either eleven or twelve my mother did leave my father. It was around Thanksgiving. She left the four of us home to fend for ourselves. I was mortified we would not have a Thanksgiving dinner like everyone else. I found a whole chicken and cooked it and made all the trimmings. Most of the food to prepare a dinner had been purchased, even though I am sure the plan had originally been to go to Wheeler Street. As I looked at the table filled with the food I had cooked, a pie I had baked, I had a sense of pride, a deep sadness and fear. "What was going to happen next?" I wondered and the most frightening thing of all, "Would anyone care?" I asked myself over and over again. I don't remember when my mother came home nor do I remember when they reconciled. Years later my Dad told me it was at about this time he was so suicidal he planned to drive his car off a cliff. I think he declared bankruptcy, which would have been totally humiliating for my mother. They were broke and did not have enough money to even pay the mortgage on the house.

I still had too much responsibility and continued to be angry and getting angrier every day. Some of my behavior continued to drive my mother crazy. I talked to myself all the time and she would lecture me endlessly, "What will people think? They might think you are crazy. You need to stop, now!" It never occurred to her that I was troubled. She would watch me as I walked home from school, babbling to myself, totally absorbed in my own conversation. And as soon as I entered the house the lectures would begin. I was so absent-minded I would leave things everywhere and put things in strange places; like the salt and peppershakers in the refrigerator. I would lose headscarves on a regular basis. I think one year I lost thirteen and I was baby sitting so I would replace them from the money I earned before she found out. Language was a challenge for me. One time I had a conversation with a neighbor lady and we begin to talk about dandruff. She asked, "Does your mother have dandruff?"

I adamantly announced, "Oh no! She doesn't have dandruff, she just has lice." When I proudly told my mother the story she went through the roof she was so upset with me. In my mind the short word was the less serious of the two.

The fighting was more frequent and the conflict between my parents was much worse. The fighting between my brothers and me was also out of control. They had stopped just taking my abuse and they fought back. Sometime in the next couple of years this tactic began to work and I quit beating on them. My youngest brother, Roy, would just explode and throw knives at me, frying pans would come flying across the room and one time he picked up an easy chair. It came lumbering across the room towards me. It was a cheap chair and fairly light and so big it was easy to dodge. My brother Elvin just stayed out of my way. Charles attacked me like a boxer, cool, methodical and with purpose. They also conspired against me. None of them caught poison oak and I did. When they went down to the creek to play they learned if they rubbed poison oak on their clothes, when I washed them, I was likely to break out with the terrible rash, poison oak. Even though I was often told I could not get it off of someone's clothes, it was clear that was exactly what was happening. It was one of those myths that prevailed regardless of information to the contrary. It was because of this conspiracy I got some of my worst cases of poison oak. I understand now what my behavior was about and no longer suffer from horrible guilt; I still feel remorse for my brothers and myself. We were barely functional. We were a wild bunch, without much guidance or direction. We learned to fend for ourselves. My brothers had each other. As the only girl and the oldest child I had no one.

    I think I was desperate to figure out how to live like everyone else. I did not have a clue. In the fifth grade I had read voraciously. In Rollingwood, books were much scarcer. The school library was non-existent; there was no public library. I read my mother's magazines. I was the neighborhood babysitter. I would willingly clean the kitchen, wash the dishes, straighten out the house, bathe the children, feed them and read to them and tuck them into bed. I was an exceptional baby sitter, except for one flaw. I would check out every closet, including linen closets, every drawer in bedrooms, in the bathroom, and in the kitchen. I snooped through all the cupboards. Sometimes when families were home and had left a window open a crack, I would sneak in the window and eavesdrop on their conversations. I was desperately attempting to understand how people lived. I knew it was different from my family. But how was it different? When I eavesdropped, sometimes I would sneak back out the window, but on occasion I would just walk into the room where the people were talking and announce myself. I don't know if anyone ever told my parents or told me to stop. I don't think I continued the behavior after I had some sense of how people lived. I was a desperate eleven-year-old.

All of us attended the local elementary school, El Portal School. Everything was still segregated. El Portal was a "white kids' school." The school was almost as weird as I was. It was during the war and teachers were scarce. The war effort and the much higher wages paid by jobs related to the war effort called to everyone. There were not enough people to fill the gaps left by the attraction of money and the pride of doing one's patriotic duty. The shortage was felt everywhere. There were not enough teachers, doctors, nurses, lawyers, clerks, plumbers, or carpenters. There was even a shortage of policemen and firefighters. This was complicated by the huge influx of people who came from all over to benefit from the bounty of California, the "Golden Land." There were way too many needs and too few resources. Some teachers who were at least in their fifties or older had never taught before. People were almost dragged off the street to teach.

When I started El Portal School, I attracted a lot of attention from the boys. I don't have a clue what that was about. I just loved it. I had never been so admired before. The girls were another story. Christine was the ringleader of the girls and I needed to unseat her or so I believed. It was my first experience with boys other than my brothers, uncles and cousins. I was overcome by this attention. I had never had this kind of attention, except for the one boy who lived across the street on Wheeler Street and that attention cost me dearly. My mother and her sisters treated me like I was some cheap little "slut." I had been so ashamed. Two very popular boys in my sixth grade class seemed to like me and I convinced them to help me and we ignored Christine and spread stories about her, until no one in class was speaking to her. I was definitely drunk on power. Then one day on the playground, she challenged me and I expected the boys to jump to my aid. Wrong, they took Christine's side. Humiliated, I stormed off the playground and went to my classroom. As I stormed down the outdoor corridor, I passed the fourth-grade teacher who stopped me and said, "I don't know what happened, but you sure deserved it." Thus ended my reign of terror.

It was in the sixth grade I learned about Spin-the-Bottle, a kissing game. I remember going to a party and we were in the garage and began to play Spin-the-Bottle. I wondered if anyone would choose me to go in the closet and kiss me. I wasn't even sure it was OK to play this silly game. Of course I did get asked. I can't say I was ever very comfortable or could get lighthearted and giggly about it like the other girls did.

Eventually things settled down. I think it helped my cause when we took the yearly IQ test and I scored in the top one percentile, as did my brother who was in the fourth grade. The fourth grade teacher called in my mother since Charles had scores so high. She wanted him to skip fifth grade. My mother refused to let him. I knew Charles was bright, and I think he knew it also. I just never knew I was bright. As for Elvin, I think he just got lost in all the chaos and violence. Roy was too young to even be considered in the equation.

In my classroom there was even a stranger phenomenon. Miss Niece, the teacher, confused me with another girl in the class, Lela was her name. Miss Niece was probably somewhere in her late fifties or early sixties. She was dithery, unorganized, and seemed more confused than her students. Her confusion was so blatant that everyone in class knew about it and laughed about it. At Christmas she gave Lela the poem, *T'was the Night Before Christmas,* to memorize. The class laughed and believed she had meant for me to memorize the poem. The day before the performance she came and asked me if I had learned the poem and I smugly responded, "You gave it to Lela to learn." She almost immediately went over to Lela, asked for the poem and gave it to me and I memorized it overnight. Lela had not even begun to memorize the poem; I think she knew what was likely to happen. It was a hurtful situation for everyone, Lela and myself. Sometimes she even mixed up our grades. I would often be the one to notice. If my grade was a C or lower I knew it was not my paper, I would check the name, talk to Miss Niece and she would collect Lela's papers and check the names and change the grade. Later it seems hard to imagine this could possibly have happened. However, when I began to teach school myself, I learned it was not as unusual a mistake as one might think.

From El Portal School I went to Roosevelt Junior High School. Miss Niece and her flighty forgetful behavior followed me to Roosevelt. I entered seventh grade. To everyone's surprise Lela had skipped seventh grade and was in eighth grade. All the kids who had come from the El Portal sixth grade to Roosevelt Junior High School was sure this was another one of Miss Niece's mistakes. Lela was as aware of all this as was most everyone else. We were all pretty helpless to do anything about it. No one had parents who did not work long shifts in the shipyards and who were even remotely interested about what happened in school. In reflecting on this it was probably better it turned out this way, but at the time I was angry and upset. Again I felt cheated out of what was mine.

While still in the sixth grade, I helped in the after school daycare for the younger children. I was considered to be too old for the daycare program, but there was no one home to take care of me. I had taken care of children since I was six years old and was perfect as a helper in the daycare. I had at least six years of experience. I think it was an exceptional program for the children with regular activities such as music, art and science. Some of the kids were served the only nutritional meal they had all day. It was certainly true for the four of us. Preparing healthy food was not high on anyone's list. Yet in many ways we ate a healthier diet than most of the kids living in Rollingwood. Poverty prevented us from eating too much sugar, pop or prepackaged food. It was the beginning of junk food.

In my home there was never any music. My first experience with music had been at Peralta, and then in the daycare center the teacher built a musical instrument using bottles filled with water to different levels. She hung them by the neck on a dowel and then tuned them by striking them with a metal rod used to strike a triangle in an orchestra. She would remove each one and add water or pour water out. I was enthralled and in awe. I thought it was beautiful and magical.

Today I can laugh at the girls in the class. We all decided to have a contest as to who could weigh 100 pounds by the end of the school year. I think I reached 99 pounds and then stretched the truth slightly. I just wanted to win something. In those days being a smart girl did not count for much. I am not sure weighing a hundred pounds counted for much, but I thought it did. What it did was give me a way to hang out with the other girls in a fun lighthearted, competitive way. I certainly did not consider myself smart and my family continued to give me no reason to believe otherwise. Within about two years I begin to worry about how fat I was. I never quit worrying until I was in my sixties.

Sometime in all of this I got my first toothbrush, began to take baths in fresh water, and had my first visit to the hospital. I would get poison oak that was totally debilitating. As I said before, in their anger, my brothers conspired and would make sure I got poison oak. Another way I would get poison oak was when my brothers played at the creek and would take our dog, Tippy, with them. I rarely played at the creek. It was too risky. I was sure to get poison oak. When I went to get my brothers to come home, I was not allowed to touch the dog since I might get poison oak. Of course that was impossible and one day when Tippy was a particular nuisance, jumping all over me, I got my second nasty case of poison oak. With the poison oak I went to a real hospital, one of the first Kaiser Permanente Hospitals. It was in Richmond. For persons who worked in the shipyards Kaiser offered health insurance. The insurance was through a contract with an insurance company. I believe for a family it was $5.00 a month. I am sure without this insurance, I would never have gone to the hospital and my mother would have figured out how to treat it herself. My face was swollen, one big weeping blister. I could not see, my eyes were closed shut, and I could not eat. I could not move. My arms were stretched straight out from my sides. Between calamine lotion, zinc oxide cream and ice-cold boric acid compresses, it gradually disappeared. I was to suffer from horrible poison oak until I was in my mid-twenties.

I had seen a dentist only once with a toothache when I was seven years old, and cried the whole time even though he barely touched me. I may have needed glasses, since sometimes I wore them and sometimes I did not. I think the school would suggest my parents get me glasses and then they would when they could afford them, but once they were broken that was it, until the school again tested our eyes and recommended glasses

During this time I started to take time off from school. I would tell my mother I was sick and she never questioned me. I usually stayed home for three or four days. I stayed in bed, read all day and slept. I ate whatever I wanted, which I pretty much did anyway. Finally I would go back to school. My mother would always write me a note.

For fun, we would take large cardboard boxes, flatten them and lug them to the hills behind Rollingwood and climb up the hill hauling our piece of cardboard, which was now a sled. On the dry summer grass we would slide down the hill, watching closely for the police, who were sure to come. They would arrive and begin warning us about fire danger. Of course the minute they turned their backs and were barely driving away, we climbed the hill and started sliding. Then the police returned and started chasing us. Sometimes someone would get caught and properly scolded or loaded into the police car and driven home. It was a real danger, but that was part of the fun, carefully watching for them and then running as fast as we could down the hill returning home. Sometimes the police won, and sometimes we did. All their warnings and the warnings of our parents never deterred us. I think we did slow down when a fire did actually get started somehow. I was not on the hill that day.

Now I took a bus to school and I went only half a day. I attended Roosevelt Junior High. I would arrive at school in time for lunch with the other freshman from San Pablo, which included Rollingwood. I had a few friends at the junior high.

School was now a whole new experience for me. The school was overcrowded and racially mixed. The tensions between the blacks and the Mexicans were palpable. Some Mexicans belonged to what I suppose were the gangs. They would cut a tattoo on their hand between the thumb and forefinger, a cross with lines shooting out of it like light rays. The threat of violence was always present. The Mexican girls wore pompadours in which, as the story went, they would hide razor blades and they knew how to use them. I don't know what the name for the girls meant, "Pachucas." I still don't know how to spell it. I remember an African American kid slapping a teacher and running off the school grounds; immediately there was a wall of African Americans surrounding the school grounds with Miss Adams the teacher in the middle. It was way too dangerous for anyone to take any kind of action. We all stood very still until the wall began to disperse. I knew about violence, but overall junior high was not too awful for me.

    I also began to express my views in social studies. I was for the communists, or for any minority group that was being maligned. I was intense and vocal. It did not last long. I think by the time I entered eight grade, I was pretty much over it. I did not stay over it.

    It was in Rollingwood that I first took total care of the family. My mother went to the hospital and I believe it was for an abortion. She was in the hospital for maybe four to five days. Years later she told me she had an abortion and a hysterectomy when I was about twelve. I cleaned the house, did the laundry, and cooked all the meals.

    By now my father's drinking and my mother's rage seemed like just a regular part of life. It was the way we lived. Yet I was determined I was going to live a different kind of life. As I reflect on the years in Rollingwood, I consider them a turning point in my life. Here I was at twelve without any idea of what the world around me was like. I was so determined to find out that I snooped, I eavesdropped, and I read *Good Housekeeping* and

McCall's. I was desperate, and in some way courageous enough to figure out how to have a life. I was going to do whatever I had to do. And in my twelve-year-old mind I had to figure out how "normal" people lived and begin in some way to act like them. I knew vaguely that they did not look like the girls in the Sears Roebuck Catalog, nor did they live like the movie stars in the movies. But they did seem to know what they were doing.

Chapter 12

HARBOR GATE, RICHMOND CALIFORNIA (1945–1950)

She climbs the ladder to the top of the barn,
Watching the old barn cat crouching, pouncing.
Carefully she walks and looks slowly at the hay
Hoping to find a fresh-laid egg.
Walking carefully, looking sharply,
Finding only six today.

It was shortly after my father and mother separated again, then reunited, that we moved to Harbor Gate, one of the many projects built in Richmond to handle the huge influx of shipyard workers and their families. They came from all over the country to build the ships used in World War II. The Richmond Housing Authority built and managed all the projects. I was probably about twelve or thirteen years old when we moved. Harbor Gate was located off of Cutting Avenue close to the San Francisco Bay. There was a big field of eucalyptus trees separating Harbor Gate from the bay. It was different from most of the projects in the area. Most of them were two stories, with about eight to twelve units in them. There was usually a central courtyard, with a sidewalk leading up to the buildings, continuing up the middle with grass on each side and small walkways going to the apartments on lower floors. At the end of the buildings there was a staircase leading to the upstairs apartments. Harbor Gate was surrounded by those projects and most likely ended up being different in order to accommodate the "white" population. The projects were segregated. The "black" population was much larger and therefore much of what had been built was to accommodate their need for more housing.

Harbor Gate was all duplexes. It was organized in an effort to separate the whites from the blacks. We did not have African Americans at that time. We had "blacks" and "whites." "Dagos and Spics." All the other projects in the area were totally inhabited by "Blacks." In my family we did not use the term "nigger," but among the people who lived around us, it was the accepted term, but it was now never used in public places. It was too dangerous!

The white families lived in the central part of Harbor Gate on the street off Cutting Boulevard. The black families lived on the edge of the project and in the back. All around our little "white" community were projects dedicated to the black population. In and around Harbor Gate, we were a minority. The biggest building on Cutting Boulevard was a large grocery store. Roy, my youngest brother told me this story. It happened on the first day we lived in Harbor Gate. My mother sent my three brothers to buy milk. It was a holiday and the big grocery store was closed. They had to cross a large lot to get to one that was open. About half way, a gang of "blacks" met them with knives, threatened them and robbed them of the money for milk. "We were mugged!" Roy proclaimed. None of them were hurt, but it left a lasting impression, as did many other such incidents.

The school bus picked us up in the grocery store parking lot and left us there when we came home. The students on the school bus were not segregated. I remember the grocery store in particular because upon arriving home, I would go into the store to the liquor counter, and buy a coke. The young man who worked behind the counter had a crush on me or so it seemed. Whenever I went to the counter, he would greet me with, "You look just like Esther Williams and, boy, is she beautiful." Then he would announce to everyone standing in the vicinity, "Hey! Doesn't she look just like Esther Williams?" In my opinion, the young man certainly was not handsome. He was a short and skinny Italian. I certainly did not want to be interested in him or have him interested in me. It was humiliating. It said something about how worthless I was when someone so "low class," unattractive and obviously not very smart was interested in me.

I was so embarrassed and annoyed. Besides, Esther Williams was the last movie star I wanted to look like. In my opinion she was only a fancy swimmer and not a "real movie star," like Lana Turner, Hedy Lamar, Elizabeth Taylor, or Rita Hayworth.

If I wanted a coke there was no way to avoid him, and I was not going to give up my coke. He endured my obvious disgust and rejection and I endured his unwanted attention. I wanted a very popular boy, like a football player or a basketball star, not a lowly store clerk.

Behind the store was the "white" section where I lived. The duplexes were made entirely of plywood, the floors, the walls, the siding, and the roof. They were heated with coal-oil stoves in the living room. The walls were eight feet square, made of plywood with minimum framing, interior walls on one side and exterior walls on the other side, with no insulation. They were nailed to the framing and then put in place.

One night during a storm the wall in my brothers' bedroom came loose and separated from the house. Roy was terrified. He came running out of the room screaming. My mother ran out into the storm in the middle of the night and pushed the wall back into place. If any repairs were done, I don't remember them. The house had three small bedrooms, one bathroom, a kitchen, dining area and a living room. The back door and the front door both opened on to a stoop. The front had a railing and a roof over it. One of my favorite things was to climb on the roof and sit there in the evening and watch the sunset over the bay and dream my dreams of the "good life."

My mother was determined to make this place better and more beautiful. She started by varnishing all the floors black and then shining them to a high gloss. She found throw rugs and put them down. She tore out a wall in the kitchen to make the dining room larger and hid the washing machine in the corner. She made valances for the living room windows, put up sheer panels, and drapes on the side. She made lampshades to match the valances and reupholstered all the furniture to also match the drapes. At some point she had worked in an upholstery shop. Upon entering the house, it looked more like a *Better Homes and Garden* house, totally unlike a simple housing project house. She used the skills she had learned from the upholstery shop, from *Good Housekeeping Magazine, The Ladies' Home Journal* and all the other household magazines she read to decorate the house. She was a brilliant, gifted and creative woman.

She then began working on the yard. She had beautiful flower gardens. She once told me the story of how she got my dad to help her with the digging. She would leave the window open close to where he might be in the house and she would work outside of it moaning, groaning and grunting, until he came out and offered to help. The story was that *Sunset Magazine* was interested in doing a feature on gardens in the projects. My mother's garden was one they had considered. I loved her flower garden. The stocks were full of a wonderful aroma, and the gladiolas stood tall and stately, then there were the Shasta daisies, roses, petunias and marigolds and much more.

Behind the house was an open space surrounded on three sides by houses and on the fourth a road and across the road the baseball field where in the spring all my Harbor Gate friends got together and played baseball. Everyone's backdoor opened on to the open space. Charles attempted to put in a vegetable garden with little success.

It was the first time in my life I really knew there were people who struggled more than we did with poverty and violence, and who were even more emotionally handicapped. Our neighbors were even stranger than we were. Across the street lived a family where all the members were mentally handicapped. In those days they were called "retarded." My mother warned all of us to stay away from them. They were rough in behavior and in their language, and so I did stay away. On one side of us lived a couple. The man was alcoholic and I did not pay much attention to them. In the other half of our duplex lived a family with two or three children. Darlene, the oldest and only girl, was close to my age. We hung out together, played baseball with the boys, and she flirted while I watched. We went to the recreation center movies together. The mother was crippled and it was a family of "yellers." We could hear them through the walls of our house and if we were outside it seemed like they never stopped.

Down the street lived a family with one daughter, Barbara. She was never part of the Harbor Gate group that hung out together. The extent of her involvement was to join us on occasion to play baseball. This family considered themselves to be much better than the rest of the families on the street. Mrs. Myers was always talking about how she could not wait to get out of Harbor Gate, out of Richmond and in fact out of California. Eventually they ended up moving to Oregon. My mother was extremely critical of Mrs. Myers and her "snooty ways." I, of course was curious, they seemed so much more organized and orderly than my family.

On the street facing ours across the field was the Berrimans' house, the last house on the street. This was a family of bizarre adults and two very damaged girls. Mrs. Berriman was always accusing her husband of having affairs and she would describe to her daughters and me, in detail, the evidence, from menstrual blood on his underwear to the fishy smell of some woman. I was often shocked. As I describe her I get that same "icky feeling" I had then, when I listened to her. But I was curious and so I would observe and watch the bickering and the fighting. One of Mrs. Berriman's favorite words was "nasty." Besides, I knew nothing about sex. When I was in the sixth grade my mother broached the subject by suggesting that surely my friends had told me all I needed to know. I hastily agreed with her. I was learning something about sex from watching the Berrimans, but nothing that would ever be of use to me.

Next to the Berrimans lived an older couple with eight kids, most of whom were grown up and gone. This family was considered to be true "Oakies" by most if not all of their neighbors. The boys in this family were particularly good looking. The Grayson family was the strangest family in our neighborhood. Mr. Grayson was an alcoholic and a wife beater. Rarely did a night pass without him yelling and screaming at someone in the family, mostly his wife and sometimes one of the kids. Often his wife would be seriously bruised. The two youngest children were girls. The youngest Billie Jo was about three years old when we moved to Harbor Gate and her sister Margie was maybe seven years old, and Dairen was thirteen. Then, there were the older boys who came and went. I knew Dairen, but not any of his older brothers. The Grayson house was the filthiest house I had ever seen. Dirty clothes were everywhere, on the couch, sometimes on the table, sometimes on chairs and even sometimes on the floor and always on the beds. It was hard to distinguish the clean clothes from the dirty clothes; they were often just mixed together. The floor was dirty and the dishes in the sink were piled high, and on the stove and on the counter and in every empty available place. Mrs. Grayson looked like she was sixty or older, but often she had blood on the back of her dress or on the slip that hung with an uneven hem about two or three inches below her dress. There were boxes in every nook and cranny. There was a path from the kitchen to the living room and then one to the hall and the bathroom. The worst part of the situation was there was always food on the table. I never saw the table without food, morning noon or night. It was the most unappetizing food I can imagine. Even the cakes she baked and the pies she made were disgusting. I don't think I can adequately describe how unappealing everything was in the house. Every time I went over to the Grayson house to visit Margie, always hoping I would magically run into Dairen, her very good looking older brother, my mother warned me, "Don't eat anything in the house, and come home to use the bathroom." The bathroom was even worse than the rest of the house. I don't think it was ever cleaned. The only other house that I remember that came near to this house in just pure clutter was my mother-in-law's house. In my family we talked about all our neighbors, and all the neighbors talked about the Grayson family.

Next to the Graysons lived a Jewish family, which was a very big deal since none of the neighbors, including my family, had ever known a Jewish family. The father was a student at Cal. He was planning to be a psychologist. His wife worked. They had two children, both under school age. I began to babysit for them. Now their house was different than any other house I had seen in the neighborhood or for that matter in my entire life. There were books, lots of books. There were art books, psychology books, and there was a record player and records. I had never been in a house where music was played I was impressed and I loved some of the music, even though I knew nothing about it. They were a quiet family. They had made an effort to have a comfortable relaxed home. It was simple and yet cozy and inviting. On the walls were prints by famous artists. Most important was they talked to each other and the parents talked to the children. They also had a group of friends that formed a community. This group of friends had all bought land in the Bay Area, having come from Los Angles. When someone was ready to build their house all of them pitched in and helped. They had parties where they would all get together and have dinner and spend the evening listening to music and having conversations. Morrie, the father, had an identical twin brother and I could not tell them apart. When I babysat I would look at the books and attempt to read them. One of the books that really attracted me was one on abnormal psychology. It scared me, but I was engrossed by it. In some way this family saved me. The friendship and spirit of cooperation among a group of friends was a whole new experience for me. In my family and among their friends it was competitive, backbiting, judgmental, gossipy, sometimes bitter and on occasion vicious in the verbal attacks on each other. Life among these Jewish families and friends looked to me more like the way life should be. I aspired to be like them. I remained friends with them for many more years.

On the same block as the Grayson family, and on the other side of the street, lived an American Indian family. The oldest was a girl my age, Donna, who had two younger brothers. Her mother had died giving birth to her on a reservation. The woman in the house was her father's second wife, not her mother, and the boys were her half brothers. Eventually, we became fast friends. We walked to the bus together. She would get in trouble with some of the other kids. She was somewhat mouthy and could be pretty defensive. One day she got into an argument with a very tough African American girl. The girl pulled out a nail file and threatened Donna. She showed the nail file and announced that if Donna ever talked to her "disrespectfully" again, it would be a knife, not a nail file. On our walk home Donna proclaimed that she could beat the girl up, "I am just as tough as she is and don't need no knife!" Fortunately, neither of them challenged the other one to prove a point. Eventually, Donna did attack her stepmother with a knife on the back and on both arms. Fortunately, she hit her on the back with the wrong side of the blade. I think it happened in our sophomore year. I went to her house to pick her up for school, and was greeted at the door by her stepmother. In a frenzy of words, Lacoma explained to me what had happened and that the agent from the Bureau of Indian Affairs had taken Donna and she did not know where she was. After school that day I went to the house of the agent, a Native American woman. It was clear she was not going to tell me where Donna was or what had happened. She also indicated I should give up on ever seeing her again.

As it turned out I did see Donna again. While I was living in Oakland and was attending what was then San Francisco State, Donna contacted me. She had called information for all the towns or cities in the Bay Area until she found me. For many years we kept in touch. She made me a turquoise ring that she had hand polished, braided the silver and then put the beautifully cut and polished piece of turquoise in the setting for the ring. After finding me she sent me the ring. A few years ago I passed it on to my grandson. She came to California once after I had moved to Grass Valley and we met at the restaurant by the turnoff to Englebright Dam and had a drink. It was a brief visit. She was in California showing her jewelry and clay work. She had shifted to clay. I saw her a second time when I went to Santa Fe to the Indian market where she was showing her clay and etched glasswork. Her life always sounded hard. She had lost a daughter to drugs, was estranged from a second daughter, and her second husband was an alcoholic. She was very tight with her son.

As the years went past, our contact became more and more sporadic. Her husband died and I could not find her. I tracked down her son and he told me how to reach her. I finally reached her, but she seemed more isolated and less willing to have contact. She was suffering from a multitude of health issues. I have not contacted her since that time. I suppose reaching out to her son to find her may have been my way of returning the favor. Not too long ago I found something she had written tucked away in some old papers. She was a bright, creative and gifted artist. She had established herself as a Native American artist. I have one piece of art from her. It is a clay piece with a very small bowl. I think it is a "Wish Keeper" and is part of her tradition as a Navajo. I am still pulled to contact her as I write this and maybe I will, but I am afraid of what I will find. I am afraid she is totally disabled or has passed away. It is hard to bear the thought of her as an old and fading woman. She fought so hard for a life and sacrificed so much to have one. Her art was her life and she stayed in a devastating marriage so she did not have to work and could just do her art. I was so touched by her efforts to find me. She was a wonderful high school friend. In some way we were both misfits, but together we could plan a life worthy of two misfits and some of our bond was because of those dreams. I am missing her.

While I was in the eighth grade I would attempt to put on plays in the living room with my brothers and the neighborhood girls. I was so very young. On Halloween I got dressed up in a costume I had made and went out "Trick or Treating." People answered their doors and made comments, "Aren't you a little old for this?" I was, and I knew it. I had never gone "Trick or Treating" and I wanted to go before I was in high school. I knew this was my last chance.

Coming from a very opinionated family, by the time I was in the eighth grade I had become as opinionated as all the rest of them. I found in social studies a platform to express my opinions and they were always on the side of what I perceived to be the underdog. I became quite vocal in my support of the communists and communism. I was filled with a fiery passion. The teacher did not hinder our fiery discussions. My earlier intensity had returned, in less than a year. My intensity and vocal protests came and went throughout the rest of my life.

When I graduated from the eighth grade, the traditional gift was a wristwatch. I knew we were too poor for my parents to get one for me. My mother, made my graduation dress out of a bright magenta moiré material; I don't know where she got it. I suspect one of her sisters gave it to her. The dress was way too old for eighth grade graduation. I was terribly disappointed by the whole event. The Saturday after graduation, I was cleaning the bathroom, when my father handed me a box. I thought it was a box of soap since we were out of soap in the bathroom. I distractedly opened the box and inside the box was another box. When I opened the box, I saw the Bulova watch box, I begin to cry. When I opened the watch box and I saw the watch, a Bulova watch, I stood in the bathroom and cried and cried. The watch meant so much to me. I understood what a big deal it was for my father to get me the watch. I don't think my mother knew what he had done because she kept talking about where did he get the money and how did he intend to pay for it. Somehow the watch was an acknowledgment that I was now a young woman. I was fourteen and I was going to high school. I kept that watch long after it had quit running.

Finally, sometime after I was married the watch disappeared in one of our many moves.

During the years in Harbor Gate I had become quite a dawdler. My mother would send me to the store and I would take an hour or two. I was never on time to anything and I ran errands at a snail's pace. Because of my behavior my mother was both constantly angry and in a state of anxiety. In her frustration and anger she would plead with my dad to do something, anything, to get me to change my behavior. Finally, out of his own frustration he decided to spank me. Mind you, I was at least thirteen by this time. I was totally shocked. I had always seen my father as my ally. I knew I was way too old to be spanked and I was humiliated and embarrassed by the whole event and angry, but not as angry with my dad as I was at my mother. I did not want to give up on my father as my ally. It took me many years to understand the nature of our relationship. I became his confidante when it served him and intervened between him and my mother often so that the fighting would not turn physical. His long-standing habit of not coming home on Friday nights and often disappearing until sometime Sunday continued until he quit drinking when I was thirteen. Even though he was working and so was my mother, we never had money. Sometimes he would come home with hat in hand and a gift of some sort for my mother to be greeted by my mother screaming, pushing him and sometimes hitting him. The ten-dollar gift was almost always the reason he had no money left. I remember him pushing her out of the way as he headed for the kitchen, barred the door with a chair, then proceed to cook bacon and eggs with my mother screaming and beating on the door. The smell of the bacon wafting under the door seemed to add to my mother's frenzy. I would attempt to stop her. "Go to bed, he is drunk. He is not going to listen to you. Go to bed. Please go to bed." And finally she did.

After he had finished eating he would sheepishly open the door and come out of the kitchen and sit on the couch and name his sins, both real and imaginary. He would sob and plead guilty to everything. After about an hour of my listening to this endless tirade, he would be too tired to continue and go off to bed with my mother. I would then look around the house, collect myself and worry about what was to come, what was next, and I would organize myself against it all in the hopes it would go away or change. When it did change, and he finally quit drinking, it did not matter; I don't think any of us believed the change would last more than a month. It lasted until he died.

Chapter 13

HIGH SCHOOL, FRIENDS, AND WHEELER STREET (1945–1950)

She heard the first rumbling roar.
There it was
The bright cracking in the sky.
She felt the drop, the second and the third.
The rumbling grew louder.
The cracking brighter oftener,
The water fell and fell.
She heard her mother's call.

In Harbor Gate we found a home for chaos. The chaos in our lives was reflected all around us, and of course we created our own fair share. Few houses escaped being impacted by the violence and unrest. Even my Jewish friends suffered. They had not been exposed to the fear and violence that lived on the streets around us. The wife hated their life and begged to move. Finally rather than get his PhD., Morrie decided to just get a teaching credential so they could move.

Elvin and Charles ran wild, Roy, the youngest, did not, out of fear. He was terrified of blood and afraid of getting hurt. Sometimes he would join them, but not always be an active participant in whatever trouble they might be creating. He was more cautious than the other two. One time when Roy was hurt and bleeding, he came running home screaming in fear.

One afternoon, my brother Charles, then nine or ten, was outside hollering for my mother, she finally got to the door and looked out and could not see him anywhere. I think her fear of a catastrophe was so overwhelming that she rushed down the stairs looking everywhere and calling his name. "Look up here, Mom," came a voice from the sky as she began to look around. Then she spotted him at the top of the telephone pole filled with all kinds of electric wires. It was bad enough that he had managed to climb to the top of the pole, but the possibility that he might be electrocuted really triggered her fear and anxiety and rightly so.

"Come down Charles, now!! You get down from there before you fall or get electrocuted or both," she yelled in a voice high with fear and with frenzy.

He came down, proclaiming, "I am fine. I know how to take care of myself. I was not going to fall or get electrocuted and fall." They stood on the street arguing briefly about who was right and of course both of them were and neither of them was. Truth is rarely black or white, even though we like to think it is.

Through the middle of Harbor Gate, close to the elementary school, were railroad tracks. Some kind of freight train would slowly travel on these tracks, probably carrying supplies for the shipyards or other industries since we were close to the industrial area. They were big, cumbersome and very noisy and fortunately slow. Of course the older kids in elementary school would attempt to hop the freight. Among them were my brother Charles and one of his friends. On a drizzly, damp day he and his friend were walking along the tracks. The train could be heard in the distance. Donald announced he was going to hop the freight. Charles warned him that the tracks and the rings on the side of the train were too slippery and wet and he would not have something he could really hold. He might slip and fall under the train. Donald proceeded with his plan and my brother watched him slip and fall under the train.

He lost his leg. Sometimes people would blame Charles for not stopping Donald. It was unlikely he could have stopped him. Some people understood that if he had tried, the accident could have been much worse and two boys could be under the wheels of that train. That accident haunted him for many years and he would ask himself those same questions that others asked or he would envision what might have happened to him if he had joined Donald.

Both Elvin and Charles, my older brothers, were wild, boisterous, challenging and intelligent guys. They had quite a reputation. When Roy, my younger brother, went to Roosevelt Junior High and followed either Elvin or Charles in a class, the teacher immediately moved him to the front of the class, or began watching him like a hawk and often he would be blamed for something some other kid did. More than one teacher would eye him and say in a voice filled with determination and caution, "Are you Elvin or Charles Leach's brother?" Roy would acknowledge that yes indeed he was. "Then get up here next to my desk and sit. I don't intend to go through with you what I went through with them."

Elvin began to hang out with some of the local young gangsters. Gangs were just beginning to form, as there was more access to drugs. The gangsters wore their Levi's barely hanging on their ass and shoes with soles an inch or two thick. Their white tee shirts had the sleeves rolled up to their shoulder to show their muscles and hold their cigarettes. Most of them carried some kind of knife, usually a switchblade. Elvin cut hose lengths and filled them with lead as his weapon of choice.

They stuck together and haunted the streets of Harbor Gate. They were the white boys and then there were the Mexican gangs and the Afro gangs. They often gambled on the elementary school grounds. One time, in broad daylight, the cops came and gathered them up to herd them into a patrol car. It was probably three or four guys. Elvin was the first to get herded into the backseat and he just went right on through and out the door on the other side. Then he walked around the patrol car, up to one of the cops and held a conversation with the cop, "Hey, what did these guys do to get themselves arrested?" He then sympathized with the cop about these "young gangsters" He was not a big guy. It was the talk of the neighborhood until the next incident where some kid pulled one over on authorities. None of my brothers reached their full height until after high school.

My brothers laughed about this story for many years. It reminded me of my uncles, who were always laughing about how they had gotten by with something or pulled the wool over someone's eyes. In many ways my brothers were like their uncles except that my brothers all worked at regular jobs, got married and settled down and had a family. Like their uncles, they all liked to gamble, drink and in general just horse around. Like their uncles, life was just a big playground and was all about having a good time. They also loved to tease. Like their uncles, they did not understand how hurtful teasing could be. They teased each other, but did not recognize that for others it could be no fun, no fun at all.

Thanksgiving the year I was thirteen was a big event. As usual we were all at Wheeler Street. The crowd at the table was smaller than usual. By smaller I mean there were fewer than twenty people. Amos, a cousin from North Dakota, was there. While in the Army he had cooked and perhaps helped in the homes of officers. He was helping to cook the dinner and introduced wine as part of the meal. In spite of the fact almost every man at the table was an alcoholic, not one of them had ever drunk much, if any, wine. Everyone was joking about being served wine. When Amos began to pour a glass of wine for my father, he stopped him and announced he had quit drinking. The jokes and kidding about the wine were nothing compared to their laughing at him, making fun of him, and teasing him about whether this was the hundredth time he had quit or more. The teasing never stopped that Thanksgiving Day. He announced he had joined AA, an organization none of them knew anything about, but it was an excuse to continue with the teasing, since they claimed they did not know there was a private club for drinkers. He did quit and he never had another drink. The last forty years of his life he remained sober and never even touched the pork chop I once cooked in a little wine.

Like everything in his life he became obsessed with AA. You might even go as far as to say he had a new addiction, Alcoholics Anonymous. The man who was our neighbor had joined some time before my father. I think he may have been my dad's sponsor. Dad went to every meeting he could find. He was gone as much as he had always been, but this time to some AA function. Needless to say, my mother was not thrilled. AA became a way of life. We went to every social event, summer picnic, Christmas Party, Easter egg hunt, pot luck, breakfast, open meeting and so it went. As much as alcohol had shaped my life, AA was now shaping it. Because of the social events my mother met wives of other alcoholics who persuaded her to attended Al-Anon. She did very reluctantly with much criticism. She did not like it and never came home happy about a meeting. She was hypercritical of the whole organization, including my father and his sponsor. It was not long before Dad was sponsoring other alcoholics.

Two incidents stand out for me. A man he was sponsoring one night shot his wife and then himself. Of course my Dad was called and went immediately. Conversation around the dinner table focused on this event and the tragedy of it. Again, it was a time when he was extremely depressed.

The second incident was a man who was an alcoholic. I overheard Dad talking about him many times. He had five kids, and they lived in a shack with not much but the four walls. Dad would tell my mother that they did not have a floor, it was just dirt. One night my father dragged all five of us, my mother included, out to go with him while he went to talk this man down from wanting to kill himself and his wife and kids. We all waited in the car. I don't really understand what we were doing there. It seems we were a family addicted to crises.

Over the years I had some resentment of AA, it was so all consuming. Again my efforts to belong and do what my friends did and to create my own life was aborted. I went to AA functions and talked AA, lived AA and breathed AA and was very grateful while I was also resentful. My social life again revolved around alcohol, this time not using it as a crutch, but AA was another kind of crutch for my dad, a healthier crutch, but still a crutch.

In the summers I continued to go to Wheeler Street to help my grandmother. Every morning she would boil coffee and put eggshells in the coffee to get the grounds to settle. While she and my grandfather drank coffee, he would give her a shot of insulin. I watched this ritual until she died. They often spoke Finnish. My grandfather would read the Finnish newspaper that came from Minneapolis about twice a week. My grandfather never said "What." He always used the word "How" in place of what. My grandmother on the other hand was very proficient at swearing in Finnish. In my family no one used the word Finnish when they mentioned the language. It was called Finn. I began to recognize her swear words before I recognized much else in Finnish. I also remember the words she used for "bad boy" or "bad girl," and I still remember the word for Finnish flat bread. Unfortunately, I don't have a clue how to write them.

My job was to cook, clean the men's upstairs bedrooms, which probably had not been cleaned since the last time I was there, which was probably Easter vacation. I was generally useful. Ethel and Florence for years had baited me to tell them horror stories about my mother. Mom and I never had a very pleasant relationship. I don't remember a time when it had been pleasant for either of us and I satisfied their perverse curiosity for years. It gave me great satisfaction for a while to inform them about how terrible she was to me. Finally I quit since I got they were just using me, not caring about me or wanted to help, but using me to be mean, critical and vicious about my mother. Ethel and her husband lived upstairs. Often she would boss me around or scold me about how I did things.

When I cleaned those two dark dingy upstairs bedrooms and the bathroom, I would find loose change everywhere. I would find it on the dresser, in their pants lying on the floor when I went through their pockets, on a nightstand, on a chair by the closet and I would keep it. I was always afraid of getting caught, but I never was. The rooms were filled with dust, the shades were always drawn, and there were dirty clothes everywhere. The musty room smelled of dirty socks, of maleness. The bathroom probably had not had the toilet, the bathtub or sink cleaned since I had done it the last time I had been there. There were always new occupants, many of these occupants had lived in these two rooms at various times, and yet it seemed like the cast of characters was always shifting and changing. When I would go to Wheeler Street to help, I would wonder who would be living upstairs this time.

My grandfather was a meat and potatoes man. One time I decided to cook spaghetti and meatballs. He would always come into the kitchen and see what I was cooking. During this time there might be anywhere from six to twenty people at the table. That night it was about nine. He came into the kitchen asked me, "What are we having for dinner?"

"Spaghetti," I announced proudly. He peered at the pots on the stove, started speaking Finnish in an angry disgusted tone, got his hat and coat and left. He was not going to eat spaghetti.

The next day when it was time to cook dinner he showed up with a pound or maybe two of stew meat. He pulled out this huge aluminum canning pot. It was probably two feet high and eighteen inches wide. The stew meat was in reality short ribs, lots of fat, bone and gristle, and not very much meat. He then told me to make stew, which of course I knew how to make. About every fifteen minutes he would come in the kitchen to see how I was doing. This stew had very little meat, lots of potatoes, some carrots and a few onions and lots of water; in fact, the pot was filled within inches of the top. He had me add cans of tomatoes and tomato sauce. He would come in to the kitchen, stir the stew, taste it, have me taste, and then tell me what a good stew it was. I never again attempted to cook anything more interesting. He was immensely pleased with himself and bragged for many years about how he taught me to make stew.

By this time my psyche was pretty fragile. My self-esteem was non-existent. All the teasing of my uncles and all the critical judgments of my mother had distorted my image of myself. I believed I was fat, which I was not. I was homely, I had a funny body, my torso was short, long legs, all out of proportion. I was horribly shy, self-conscious, lacking in social skills. My hair was thin, my mouth was big with protruding teeth and I was way too tall. I didn't look like any movie star or have any redeeming physical qualities, and besides I was so poor I could not even dress right. All of this was much worse than the fact that I also believed that I was stupid. I could bear being stupid, but not being pretty or having a "figure," meant it was unlikely I would ever have a boyfriend. I was so lonely and I believed a boyfriend would really save me, but it was unlikely anyone would want me. In my teenage mind, I was doomed. At school I did not belong to any one group. I hung at the edges of all the different groups.

A girl, whose mother had some position at the school, informed me I was in the gifted group. My very first thought was someone had made a mistake and when they found out about the mistake they would move me to the lowest group. When the year went by and I did not get moved I decided I was at the bottom of the gifted group. I doubt I had much awareness what it meant to be part of the gifted group.

As I said previously, in those days they practically would drag teachers off the street. Richmond had grown from a very prestigious small high school in a small city to one with close to two thousand kids. Most of school I actually loved. Miss Webber my English teacher appreciated my writing, but not my spelling or grammar. I loved art appreciation and French and the teachers who taught them. Miss. Gremmer shared all her stories of visiting Europe and I developed a strong desire to see places like the Louvre, the Sistine Chapel, the great cathedrals, art galleries, and go to the opera and concerts. I wanted to travel, especially to Italy and France, and maybe Germany and England. A whole new world was opened to me, a world I barely knew existed except through the horror stories of the Second World War.

I liked PE and I got along relatively well with the other kids. I knew which ones to totally avoid and which ones were either "in" or close to "in." We embroidered our names on the pocket of our blouse and on the leg of our shorts. My first initial and my last name spelled Bleach and thus one of the P.E. teachers called me "Bleach." We would all be standing in line and she would call out our names. It took me a while to recognize, "Bleach" as my name. For some reason I decided I wanted to run for a school office in my junior year. I decided to run for Girls' Athletic Director. At the assembly I needed to demonstrate a cheer. It was terrible. I was way too scared. I don't even think I thought I would win, but it was probably the only office, in my mind, where I had any chance at all of winning. I did not win.

I was required to take algebra and the teacher had a reputation as an old warhorse and for me that was exactly what she was. It did not take much to scare the pants off me and she did. I actually think I would have liked algebra if I had had a different teacher.

I took chemistry and cheated on a test and then I could not stand it and I confessed to the teacher, Mr. Fischer. In my second year of chemistry we were doing experiments. Mr. Fisher was not a good teacher, but he was a good chemist and was sober. The second semester of chemistry we had a new teacher, Mr. Perry. He was neither a good teacher nor a good chemist and he was rarely sober. He had a lab assistant. Mr. Perry would spend most of his time in the storeroom sleeping or, as most of the class believed, either recovering from a hangover or creating one. That year while doing an experiment, mine blew up and the liquid flew everywhere, hitting a friend in the face. I was beyond mortified. I was totally devastated. Fortunately, it did no damage, but it could have blinded her or scarred her. Mr. Perry moved faster than anyone ever imagined was possible. I decided I was not a scientist or a mathematician.

It was not until I went to college that I developed a love of math. When I was taking teacher education classes, I was amazed to learn it was actually much more than computation. I fell in love with math theory. I also begin to have a relationship with science, and found it equally fascinating.

I loved geometry. Mr. Phelps had quite a reputation. If you needed help or a good grade you should wear a low-cut dress or blouse. You were assured plenty of help as he leaned over your shoulder. Sometimes some of the girls would sit with their legs spread right in front of his desk and then laugh as they watched him leer. I still loved geometry. I was embarrassed by all the sexual innuendos.

Are any of the stories I heard about teachers true? I really don't know. Was the old PE teacher really queer, whatever that meant? Was Mr. Perry a drinker and Mr. Phelps a letch and did Mr. Pascoe challenge acting out boys to a wresting match and then beat the hell out of them? I don't really know. I do know the school staff was in over their heads. Knife fights, racial tensions, gang fights and students who just came to school to cause trouble were fast becoming the norm rather than the exception. Students were shot and killed, mostly while off the school grounds, and sometimes someone was stabbed and died.

During my junior year the Bureau of Narcotics did an assembly about drug use, showing horrible pictures of the effects of heroin. They talked about using marijuana as the drug that always leads to much more serious and stronger more addictive drugs. They informed us that the use of heroin had almost been eradicated and would totally disappear within a couple of years. They claimed to have won the battle in ridding the United States of heroin. Later that year the little grocery store across the street was raided and closed. A gang of kids from the high school was caught smoking marijuana. Even then I knew big trouble was on its way.

The costume of the day for girls was long, very tight skirts that came down just above your shoes to the lower calf and sweaters in the winter and full skirts and peasant blouses in the summer. With the long tight skirts the walk was some sort of shuffle or hobble. I had one coat all through high school and it was a red swing jacket that hit me just below my hips.

I wore this red coat fall, winter, and spring when I was having my period. I dreaded my period. We did not have to play PE when we were having our period. I would go to the bathroom and check between every class to make sure the little hooks with small sharp teeth that hung down from the belt around my waist were still holding the pad in place. I made sure I was not leaking anywhere. I hated that everyone knew when you had your period, since you were not, under any circumstances to dress or participate in PE. I was sure all the boys knew the story. I was probably right that some of them did, and for me it was a very big and disgusting deal. It never occurred to me that wearing my red coat only at certain times might have been a dead giveaway.

    The "in" shoes were white bucks; the desired brand was Spalding, because they had red soles. The shoes were made from leather or suede, called "buck." Then either the buck or the leather was polished to a blinding white. It was rumored that in order to get them white enough you needed a whole bottle of Ace white shoe polish and you went over the shoes several times to create the correct look. It meant you used one bottle of white Ace shoe polish every single night. Everyone wore bobby socks and how the sock was rolled down identified the high school you attended. At Richmond High School socks were large rolls sitting on top of the shoe. No space to show any sock and then the roll. The rule was shoe and roll. El Cerrito girls wore socks rolled in a very tiny roll just above the ankle. For Berkeley the roll was tiny but like Richmond it was rolled down below the ankle and sat on top of the shoe. Throughout the Bay Area I could identify where each girl I saw went to high school by her socks. Did everyone else pay attention? I don't know, but I did.

    My clothing budget went for school clothes, not pajamas or underwear. My bras were often held together with safety pins and my underwear was thin and worn. Once I lost my bra at the makeshift movie theater at the recreation center. It just fell to pieces and slipped down around my waist. Eventually I took it off in the dark and let it drop to the floor. I improvised everything else. I did not get the right shoes, but the ones I had, I polished diligently and was always disappointed. My mother and I made all my skirts in the winter and all my full skirts and dresses in the spring. The style was to wear a blouse with a Peter Pan collar under a sweater and an eighteen-inch string of pearls. If you were popular and had Spalding shoes, you also had cashmere sweaters, and blouses with decorated collars. Your clothes came from Capwell's in downtown Oakland. Shopping at a thrift store was considered worse than terrible. I could not afford blouses so I bought a dickey at Sears to wear under my sweater. I don't remember having more than one. A dickey is a piece of cloth that you can tuck into the neck of a sweater with a collar attached to it. I was never going to own eighteen-inch pearls so I had a very cheap pearl necklace, but it was much shorter, more like a choker. I am sure no one had expensive or real pearl necklaces. I pinned the necklace under the collar so it appeared to be much longer than it was. It took me a long time to figure out how the popular girls got the roll on their socks so big. Finally a friend informed me they stuffed cloth in them and then rolled them. That is how I remember the state of high school fashion. It did change, and Peter Pan collars disappeared and so did extra tight long skirts, sweaters that ended at the waist and, of course, the pearls. By the time I graduated from high school pleated skirts with long nubby knit sweaters were the rage. Aunt Evelyn took me on my very first shopping trip to Capwell's where I got a nubby knit sweater and one pleated skirt. I was in heaven. Jeans rolled up to just below our knees topped with our father's white shirt, if he had a white shirt, was even a more important outfit than the Capwell's outfit. Of course, jeans and dad's old white shirts were never allowed in school. You could tell a "cheap girl" by her pierced ears.

Many things were not allowed in high school that are now almost standard wear. Sundresses, low cut dresses, short dresses, pants of any kind and, of course, shorts were definitely not allowed. Dangling earrings were not allowed or too much jewelry. I view it as an effort to make us homogenous, to make us all fit in the same little box.

My high school years were fractured and my life was split among the kids who played baseball together: my friendship with Donna, my American Indian friend, the Berriman girls, the Jewish family, Wheeler Street and the kids with whom I attended class.

Chapter 14

GROWING UP, LEAVING HOME
(1946–1950)

*She heard the "don't" and the "careful" in her head at night
And cried in alarm, terrified with fear!
No one came to comfort her or cared about her fear.
She huddled more deeply lost to the world behind her fear,
Too scared to risk the world's dangers that played in her head.*

    Darlene and I played baseball with a gang of boys who lived around our street. It was among my most fun times. Fun was hard for me since I was so damned self-conscious. I learned to ride a bicycle for the first time and I rode it with these same kids. My bike did not have anything but the metal piece as pedals. One time I fell and the end of the pedal stabbed my leg deep enough to have my parents insist I needed to go to the hospital. I locked myself in the bathroom and refused to come out until they both promised they would not make me go.

    Among those kids on the street, my family had a certain amount of prestige. We were the first family to own TV. Everyone would flock to our living room after school and watch TV. Then somehow a ping-pong table was added to the mix and our living room became a hangout. The furniture in the living room was pushed back out of the way to make room for the TV and the ping-pong table. I don't know how long it lasted, probably until my father was no longer obsessed with AA and he became a rather grumpy guy.

I was kept safe, especially when Donna picked fights with African Americans and they all knew I was her friend. Ona Carpenter, an African American girl, would walk me home after school. Safety was an important issue. I think it was an effort on her part to keep me safe. It worked. I also think we liked each other. I had two African American friends, Ona and Evelyn. During this time there was a big movement to again segregate the schools. A strike of all the white kids was organized. A large group decided not to go to school until the schools were again segregated, as they had once been many years before. My mother was a person who believed in most of the liberal causes and was strongly opposed to segregation. We went to school. She believed in the Democratic Party, in Roosevelt, in the causes of the unions and all of the New Deal. She was vocal, but not an activist.

Those years were also my first attempt to change anything. I actively became involved in the recreation center in Harbor Gate and attended meeting after meeting to get more activities, more places for kids to talk. I planned and organized dances even though I often did not attend them. I ended that involvement when some kid was shot at a dance. It was kept quiet, but stories like that were hard to keep quiet. I also joined Christian Endeavor, a Christian group for teens. Here, I was a strong active leader. A Reverend Hyde started it. One night he disappeared with a stash of money from the little church he had started and any funds that the CE group had. No one ever saw him again. I was pretty disillusioned and stopped those efforts.

I was the only teen who spent any time at the Browns'. I spent as much time there as I could muster. They had two children much younger than I was. I was impressed that these kids had chosen the paint for the walls and all the decorations for their rooms. They were different from any of the kids I knew. They liked books and games and talking. The boy could be mean and he was brilliant. He grew up to be a math wizard, got a PhD, and taught at University of Hawaii. The girl in the family married a man who from what I observed took a long time for the family to accept. I maintained some kind of contact with this family until after I was married and had moved to Red Bluff. I dated a young man whose family were the best friends of the Browns. This was a long time after I had graduated from high school.

The Berriman family was another story. I think I was trying to save those girls. I had little in common with them. The parents both often shocked me. In the five years I was around the family shocked me by the emphasis on sex and sexual acting out. Mr. Berriman never entered the house, and I mean never, without his wife accusing him of being unfaithful. The overt sexual language, the raw and graphic words and the meanness between the parents never failed to shock me.

One time Arlene the oldest girl wanted to have a party for some reason, and I don't remember the reason. This was a bare house, with not much of anything. I was helping her plan it and helping with the food. It became clear that she did not a have a tablecloth, napkins, enough dishes, silverware or even chairs. We emptied my house, carrying armloads of stuff to the Berriman house in order to create the kind of atmosphere we had seen in *Good Housekeeping* magazine. It became a common occurrence. I was always helping someone organize a party. One time we even took the dining room table over to someone's house for a party. Finally, my mother got so angry, I stopped. Most of these parties happened while she was at work and did not know what was happening. It was very strange to be the one with more.

I suppose my most striking and appalling memory of this family was when Aileen got her first boyfriend, a young man home from the service. Aileen was not terribly interested in him, but he hung out and made it clear he wanted to date her. He was not what one would consider a particularly attractive man. He had flaming red hair, protruding teeth and was long and thin. One day he came over to the Berriman house to see Aileen, and

I was there. Mrs. Berriman joined us and showed a great deal of interest in Red, as he was known in the neighborhood. Finally she said to him in her cloying, syrupy voice, "Come with me, I want to show you something," as she led him into the bedroom. We waited and waited for them to return. Finally Aileen decided to peek in the window to see what was happening. She went out to the front yard to peek into the large bedroom window facing the street. She came back in the room, her face pale and filled with fear and horror. She just said, "They're doing it." We both knew what "doing it" was.

The tension in our house never quite disappeared even though my dad had quit drinking. He was now a "dry alcoholic." He was grim, angry, guilty, and overcome with self-pity to such a degree we were all pretty miserable, my mother most of all. For the second time my mother needed to go in the hospital for surgery. The first time was in Rollingwood. I kept the house, cooked and cleaned. The second time, while we lived in Harbor Gate, was for a hysterectomy. While she was gone, I washed all the windows, the curtains, scrubbed and waxed all the floors, cleaned out the closets, cupboards and all the shelves. I washed and ironed all the clothes. I rolled up the rugs in order to clean, scrub and wax the floors. I cooked for my father and brothers. She was gone for a week and I was determined that the house would be perfect for her. My father went to bring her home from the hospital. I was so excited and thought she would be thrilled. Her only comment was, "MY GOD! What have you done to my curtains?" I kept on trying.

I wanted my mother to notice me and appreciate me. I worked diligently, plotted and planned in order to get her approval and appreciation. I never felt I got any, but I still kept on trying and trying. During the Rollingwood and Harbor Gate years, I made sure we remembered my mother's birthday. Not just me, but I reminded my brothers and my father so they would not forget, or I bought all the presents for everyone to give to her. At Christmas, my parents would give me everyone's gifts to wrap including mine and tell me not to look at it. I never looked at my gift. I think I wanted the same thrill that I saw in everyone else's face. When I was eighteen I wrapped my only present, a dark-pink wool suit.

I still spent time at Wheeler Street helping. One afternoon when I was fifteen I saw the movie, *The Snake Pit*, starring Olivia De Havilland, about insanity and institutions. I was sure I was as crazy as the woman in the movie and equally sure I needed to be in an institution. I quit eating and could not sleep. I lay awake night after night sure that I was crazy and would suffer the same fate as the woman in the movie. I don't know how long this lasted, but to me it seemed like it was forever. One night, late, in sheer desperation, I phoned my mother, crying on the phone, "I am going crazy and I am so scared."

Her response to me was to yell, "Cut it out, pull yourself together and don't talk or think such nonsense." I don't think the conversation was much longer than that. It certainly was not what I wanted, and yet it may have been what I needed, since I did exactly that. I don't think I was magically cured, but I did know never to reveal anything about myself again. And I never did for many years.

I decided to read the Bible. I had very little real experience with religion. While we still lived on Wheeler Street, I was invited by a family at Peralta School to attend Sunday school with their daughter. I went for a while, how long I don't really know. My second experience with religion was when we lived in Rollingwood and another family invited me to attend church with them and their daughter. But this time it was a Pentecostal Church. I probably went about two times. All my experience with religion was through the viewpoint of Aunt Hilda or Christian songs sung and played on the piano by Ethel and Ervin. I began reading the Bible and thinking all the "beget"s and "bigat"s were a waste of time. I was determined to read it every day and to read it from cover to cover. I think over a period of time I probably read it through a couple of times in bits and pieces. Of course I skipped all the "beget"s. I began to kind of back off from reading it until one night I was awakened by a very short dream. The dream was an auditory dream. It was a voice calling to me. "The book, the book, the book." I took up reading the Bible again for a short while and continued to do so every several years, off and on. Many years later I had another dream, but this time the dream was about how important the word "beget" is. For me it meant it connected us not only to all of our history, but also how we are all connected. It meant for me there was some meaning to be learned from our history and what we could heal in ourselves healed not only the past, but also the present and the future. It was a very powerful awareness. I think my explanation here is over simplified, yet I also think there is truth in it.

I had my first boyfriend in my freshman year. We had known each other just a short time when he asked me to go to a movie. I thought he would be OK as a boyfriend, certainly not as handsome as the Grayson boy, but good enough. Just before our date he was fishing in a boat on the bay and there was some kind of accident and he drowned. I was shocked and in my magical-thinking way, decided it was a sign. I would never have a boy friend.

In my junior year I had my first serious boyfriend. I really don't know how it happened. I was so painfully shy and self-conscious. I took drama that year and played the siren in the play, "Meet Me in Saint Louis." It was while I was in the class I heard that some of my classmates might have been interested in me if I had not been so darn shy. No one was more surprised than I was.

The young man, Jack, who lived one street over, and his friend, Herb, took an interest in me. They were high school graduates, Jack had a car and they wanted to spend time with me. I was riding high. They would come by my house to get me to go for a ride. One time they brought a friend from Berkeley and I was definitely attracted to him. I began to go places with Dan without Jack or Herb. Dan had graduated from Berkeley High School. The things Dan had going for him were that he was not from Richmond, he did not live in a project, he was tall and had black wavy hair and he could sing. He also had his own car, a black Plymouth. What was against him was that he lived in Berkeley, which was too far away and he was a gunsmith. He made guns. He worked in a little shop on University Avenue. The worst thing about him was he liked making guns better than he liked me.

I don't remember that we did much but go for a ride and I would get him to sing and then we would park and neck. When we went out on a weeknight and had no particular plans, I would often have my hair wound into tight flat curls secured with and fastened down with bobby pins. My head would be covered with these flat little curls and then covered with a scarf tied either on top of my head like "Rosie the Riveter" or by a scarf folded into a triangle and tied at the base of my neck. These curls were called "pin curls." Sometimes, my hair would dry while we were driving around and sometime not. When it dried I took out the pins and combed out the curls. During hunting season we did a lot of parking on weekdays. On weekends Dan would be off hunting with his boss. A favorite place to park was the Berkeley Marina, "making out" or "necking" as it was then called. I had my hair in pin curls, we were in the backseat, when the light shined on my face and my pin curled head. I was mortified. The officer was pleasant enough and ordered me back into the front seat. Then he suggested Dan take me home and leave me at home the rest of the evening.

I dated Dan the rest of my time in high school. He took me to the senior prom. I introduced a friend of mine to a friend of his and they started dating. Eventually they got married and moved to Fresno where he bought an exterminator business. I did not have a clue about relationships. All I knew was from movies and from my family. As I watched my friend, Joan, with Dan's friend I was amazed. She was definitely in charge and it was his job to please her. I had it backwards; I thought I should try to please him.

I remember very few things about dating in high school, but I do remember that if a young man came over to see me, I had to watch my mother flirt with him and he would pay more attention to her than to me. One time when Dan came over to the house to pick me up, my mother, being her usual self, engaged him in a lengthy conversation. Finally we got out the front door. When we got in the car Dan announced, "You know what I thought when your mother was visiting with me? To hell with Beverly, I am going to date her mother." Dating for me was a lot of things, but rarely fun.

My brothers were, from what I could see, totally out of control. My father was not around much. I attempted to talk to my mother about it. Or I yelled at her about it and attempted to get her to do something. Anything. She sat in a rocking chair and rocked and knitted and never spoke to me, yelled at me or talked to me. It was like I was not there. Our relationship was increasingly stormier. I had made a few good friends at school and if she met them or saw me with them she would be critical of them, put them down and tell me how bad they were for me. This happened even when she had met them only once. It did not matter what I did; it was never good enough. I was cleaning my brothers' bedroom at that time. They complained that I was going in their bedroom to snoop, and I was. I felt like I had won major battle when my father informed them that as long as I cleaned their room and they did not, I had a right to do anything I wanted in their room and if they did not like it, then they needed to clean their room and keep it clean.

I had been teased so much while growing up among my mother's family that in any group I was teased. I actually thought it was the way people related. I was often the scapegoat at home, at Wheeler Street and in the neighborhood. By neighborhood I mean my baseball-playing friends. I was not an early riser. One morning as I came out of my bedroom in my little shorty nightgown and looked toward the living room here were all these guys, friends of my brothers attempting to look nonchalant. The next step I took I felt something under my foot. I looked down and here was a dead snake stretched across the hall and I was stepping on it. I screamed and screamed. I wanted to kill my brothers, but stormed back to my bedroom in the midst of a storm of laughter. No one came to my defense, neither my mother nor my father. Even if they were not there, when I told them about it they just nodded their heads and went on finishing their dinner at the dinner table that night.

It still amazes me what my mother could do with a pound of meat and stretch it to feed six people. We ate a lot of ground beef and macaroni. Sometimes we ate hamburger patties with potatoes and vegetables. We often ate stew; spaghetti was another staple, as was fried chicken and one time the rabbit my brother killed. We ate scalloped potatoes or macaroni and cheese. If we had dessert it was often a quart of Neapolitan ice cream that came in a rectangular box. It was carefully measured and cut into six slices. If my mother cooked a steak, which was rare, it was cooked to shoe-leather-like consistency. Yet, it was the most acceptable way to prepare meat. A very special treat was when Dad would come home with a three-by-eight-inch block of milk chocolate about two inches thick. The whole block would be gone in one sitting.

When I took in ironing to make some money and it sat for over a week, damp and rolled up, I was told to get it ironed immediately and then I also got one of Dad's lectures about responsible behavior. I had an autograph book for people to sign and write little sayings or notes. They were very popular and many kids in high school had these little autograph books. I asked my father to write something to me and he agreed. This is what he wrote, "Dear Daughter, Everything in its place and a place for everything. Love Dad"

I had also begun designing clothes, not necessarily making them but designing them. I knew how to sew, but what I was designing was way too sophisticated for high school fashion. My parents had some friends who seemed rather impressed with my designs. They offered to pay for me to attend a fashion design school and to help me open my own boutique in San Francisco. I really did not believe them and I was probably right, no one in my family had that kind of connection with anyone who had enough money to do what this couple was promising. I paid very little attention to what they offered. Big influences for me on the good life remained Hollywood, *Good Housekeeping*, *Vogue* and *Seventeen*, a girls' magazine.

After Dad quit drinking, his addiction shifted to perfection at all cost. There was never enough money and the tension between my parents was exhausting. Shortly after I graduated from high school, the tension spilled over and my dad left for Oregon. He and my mother had split up yet again. Over the years when my parents separated, my dad would write me these horrible letters, very similar to his Wheeler Street lectures. The letters were full of how awful he was, how regretful he was and always a request everyone's birthdate and correct age so, "I can be sure and remember them with a proper birthday gift." These proper birthday gifts never arrived. Finally I was done with his letters. I never wanted to see any of them again. I gathered them all up and planned to burn them in the incinerator barrel. I was on a roll and I did not stop with just the letters. I had a yellow dress I had made that I decided was bad luck. I had made it and whenever I decided to wear it, nothing seemed to work out as planned. I took all my dad's letters from over the years, read them, took the yellow dress and the letters out to the barrel used as an incinerator, tossed it all in the barrel, lit a match and burned all of it. I was immensely proud of myself, a little sad and quite relieved.

Eventually my father came home. He had stayed someplace in Oregon with his dad in some dingy rundown hotel. My grandfather got into a poker game and was on a real winning streak. Like most winning streaks it shifted and he began to lose until he was broke, but was convinced if he just had some more money or something to bet, his luck would turn again. He took all my father's possessions and his old beat-up car and lost all of it in the poker game. To my mother's relief that incident ended Dad's relationship with his father. Somehow he got a job in Prineville, Oregon, and of course my parents reunited. For my mother it was another place where life might magically change and be her "Golden Land." My parents and my brothers moved to Prineville, Oregon.

They waited long enough to see me graduate from Richmond Union High School. I took a few suitcases of things and carried my high school diploma, with my name written on the cover in gold, Beverly Joyce Leach, under my arm and I moved back to Wheeler Street. I had a job working at the dime store, Kress, on Shattuck Avenue in Berkeley. I was determined to marry Dan. I weighed less than I had ever had in my life. I lived in one of the bedrooms upstairs on Wheeler Street. My grandparents lived downstairs and Aunt Ethel and her husband Jack lived in the upstairs apartment.

Life was familiar and in that familiarity I felt safe. I was making money, I was in "love" and I was thin. I was determined to marry and have a family. Best of all I was thin. I had no intention to go to college. It never entered my head as a real option. I was sure my life was on the "right track." I was like everyone else. All the girls I knew planned to marry and have a family. I walked like an adult woman, I talked like an adult woman and I even looked like one, but in reality, emotionally, I was probably about five years old. Was I the exception? No, I don't think I was.

Chapter 15

CONCLUSION

She hears her mother's call, does not want to answer.
But she knows she hears the don'ts and carefuls in her head during
the long nights. Crying in terror turns to anxiety!
No comfort, no one to care about her littleness,
Being overcome with fear.
Now I know where she hides.
Huddling quietly, behind her fear, lost to the world.
Afraid to risk, the world too big, too dangerous.
No guidance, no support, only loneliness.

I wanted to write this story originally for the many people who have shared their pain and suffering with me. I have been privileged to witness their growth, change, and their rediscovery of their human beauty. As a therapist, I have seen often how they got stuck in their beliefs, that something was terribly wrong with who they were. They blame themselves, they never forgive themselves, and they continue to live in shame and humiliation. Sometimes they have buried all of this so deep they can pretend it does not exist. Human beings can hold secrets so close in their hearts, they can barely feel them anymore and yet those secrets, the shame and humiliation, are running their lives as surely as the stories they make up and tell themselves. For the sake of their survival, they wear a mask or live in hiding or isolation so what they believe to be the truth about themselves can never be seen. Underneath they are filled with self-hate and self-loathing. They feel it must be their fault, if only they had been good enough they would be loved, by parents, grandparents, aunts and uncles. If they had been good no one would have hit them, no one would have abused them, there would have been plenty of food, shelter and clothes. They lived in the magical thinking of the hurt child.

If only someone had said, "Good job," "You look pretty today," "You are a good helper, the way you held the board for me was just right." If someone had delighted in them, listened to them, and looked at them and just smiled. There would be enough love, empathy, appreciation and delight in the fact that each of them was here. Having gotten enough in their souls, each would know without a doubt, "I am enough."

With each person, I reminded myself what it has been like for me to sit in the clients' chair for so many years with my own struggle to peel the layers off until I found my deeper self. Sometimes now I still think I need that special one person who is there just to listen to me. This child got so little.

Often things we do for others are really a gift to ourselves. This story may be a gift to others, and I hope it is. I know it is a gift to me. First, it was a shock to write it, one episode after another until a childhood was done. For this child there was not much of a childhood. I was asked to be an adult way too soon, much too young.

As I wrote I reached a new understanding of my own behavior and my suffering. I grieved for all the ways I took care of myself when no one was there, and all the ways I took care of others in the hope I might be loved. I struggled to figure out how to create a life and understand how others lived. It was painful and hard work. I recognize my own courage. It was shocking to see how early life-long patterns were established. The story of the scapegoat began at birth and lived in me for many years. My struggle with others began in a home of chaos and was exacerbated by the people in my family who teased me, made fun of me and laughed about how I looked, my intelligence or how I behaved. My sense of not being wanted left me distrustful, overly cautious, but mostly with no social skills, no way of knowing how to belong or how to protect myself.

My curiosity saved me and defended me. It was very important to know what was going on everywhere in the world around me, in every little corner, crack and cranny. Thus I became a curious child who grew into a nosy, intrusive adult. I had to know because if I didn't and I could not control it I might die, be tortured, or my soul would be murdered.

In order to hide my neediness, I have been overly generous, not wisely generous or generous without deeper motives. I was generous to avoid the appearance of needing anything. I did not believe and sometimes still don't that anyone would ever be there for me. I used hiding who I truly was to avoid being seen as the needy, small being I felt like I was.

My struggle with most of these defensive structures kept me alive and functioning. Over the years I began to uncover them and work with them until I was in charge, not my wounds, or scars. Have they changed or gone away? No, I can't say they have, but I know them well and I know when they creep into my behavior and the struggle to recognize them without shame or judgment. The difference is awareness, acceptance and gratitude. At one time I needed these structures to just remain on the planet, I am grateful to them for my very life. There could be no gratitude without awareness and acceptance. They would have remained buried and still in charge. Now I can say, "Thank you for all you did to help me and keep me here, I know you had my best interests and because of your help I had the opportunity to really look at who I am. I no longer need to count on your presence. Now I know, I can count on myself to keep myself safe and to love, be compassionate and grateful for who I am. I can appreciate myself. I can even love what I deemed to be unlovable."

I avoided commitments to any one thing. I was a member of many groups at once, on the edge. I became very perceptive and intuitive, to stay safe. For me the world was a dangerous place. I roamed between groups, when I was standing still and in my mind to other places. I avoided my own pain, deep hurt, rage and grief by roaming, by being curious, by being a caretaker and under all of this was fear, pure, overwhelming fear. I believed my birth was a mistake and I did not belong here. I was often suicidal.

Most important, I learned that all my behavior, no matter how weird, how destructive it appeared, how inappropriate, how humiliating it was, was an effort to save myself, to live and I think to live until I could heal myself, each little bit by each little bit. I think I was very fortunate that I survived since some of my behavior was downright dangerous, thoughtless and often mean, but somewhere in my being it was to keep me alive. I believe those who have sat in front of me over all these years were just trying to keep themselves alive.

One of the most important lessons I learned and struggle to practice is that most of the things I hated in myself and wanted to keep secret were nothing more than human struggles, human troubles: being pregnant when it was totally the wrong time to have a baby, marrying for the sake of marriage or belonging, being in the wrong relationship, and then using all of this to confirm my opinion that I was bad. I did everything in my power to look right. I worked to be thin, to be smart, to be sophisticated and to catch up with everyone I knew. All my life I had fewer social skills than I needed. My education was dismal and inadequate. I attended too many schools and too many inadequate schools. My experiences were limited.

Most important, the more I revealed about myself the less I hated myself. The less I hated myself, the less I judged others and myself. If I could love the struggling human I am, I could love the struggling human you are. I don't need to pretend and I don't need you to pretend to be anything but a vulnerable, limited human.

Being able to write all of this in the most honest way I could has touched me deeply and brought tears to my heart. I am proud of what I have created in my life. I am touched by the experience of love and care. Often, I still feel overwhelmed. This is a good life, a meaningful life and a life that is being well lived and appreciated with joy, happiness and gratitude most of the time. I don't even want it to be all the time, since I want to be engaged in life and all that it is: sorrow, joy, grief, and yes, anger, despair and disappointment and of course those precious moments of deep happiness and delight. I love coming to terms with being ordinary. What delight, freedom and joy that has brought me.

I love the earth and all who inhabit this beautiful place. I attempt to treat all things with love and respect. Am I perfect in my efforts? No, of course not, I am a being in progress. I want to remember to savor life: the sour, the sweet, the bitter and spicy.

Once a child watched the earth turn golden, then brown.
Listening to the rustling sounds she loved,
She saw the wind swaying the wheat.
She knew no swaying blue ocean.
She saw a leaf flutter toward the ground,
Her body filled with sadness, the loss she felt,
But was a mystery in her mind.

ACKNOWLEDGMENTS

I would like to thank all the teachers at Peralta School for knowing the true meaning of teaching was in the relationship, not in the content. I would especially like to thank Miss Geary, my fifth grade teacher, who gave me the greatest gift of all, her faith and care. I learned to read in the fifth grade.

I want to thank Miss Webber, my high school English teacher who believed I could write, even if I could not spell, punctuate or remember all the rules of grammar.

I would like to express my gratitude to the women of La Vulva. We met, we read our writing, shared our paintings, our poetry and our off-the-wall creative ideas. The group no longer meets. I want all of those women to know how much I love them, admire them, respect them and I am deeply grateful to them. They gave me so much.

I am grateful to Donna Hanelin, a writer, artist and a friend who taught writing classes in Grass Valley for many years. It was in those classes I began to write again after over a forty-year hiatus. I miss her presence in Grass Valley.

I also want to thank Molly Fisk, who after listening to me, reading what I wrote, supporting me, and encouraging me and after editing this book, may totally agree with my high school English Teacher, Miss Webber. I am grateful for her skill, for her coaching and her ability to laugh. I am relieved that if she had any judgments about my writing, or the book, she kept them to herself and managed to survive all my insecurity, fear and anxiety. I came out of the experience with a tender place in my heart, Molly. Thank you so much!!

To my family who can tell you horrible stories about me and who survived my weird sense of humor. I love them dearly and feel loved by them. I am so grateful for my grandchildren: Caitlin, Taylor and Nicole, they are all a delight in my life and I am especially grateful to Ava for being born and for being my great-granddaughter.

To my brothers, who swear they had a different experience than I had growing up, yet this is also their story and at the same time not their story.

I have a fabulous group of friends, bright, interesting, supportive and fun. They have all enriched my life, helped me grow and been there for me when I needed help and could not ask. They also have called on me to behave better than I was ever capable of doing. I want to thank Nina Krebs, Beulah Amsterdam. Phyllis Watts and Jackie Horn. Thank you: Karen and Doug Baer, Rich and Joey McCutchan, Nina and Dave Krebs, Candence and Gordon Little, Stephanie Zack, Peter LaFortune, Penny Fable, Myra and Mic McPherson, Jack and Cindy Love, Joyce Wilson, Dodie Johnston, Julie Cobden, Lynette Smith James, Lois Mendonca, and Ginny Griffing. I also want to thank Susan Suntree, a gifted artist who always knew how much I wanted to write, paint and be creative, and in her wisdom never laughed or discouraged me. And all those I did not remember. To all those remembered here and those who are not, you are all so dear to me.

I could not write this without remembering those very special people who I love and are no longer with us; Eve Hall, Teddy Kell Emrich, and Mary Bolton.

Above all, thank you to all the people who sat across from me and shared so much of themselves and helped me to look at myself and to grow. I especially had you in mind when I wrote this. You enriched my life, humbled me and as I watched you blossom, my faith in myself and in all of us grew and grew.

If I remembered everyone I hold with warmth, love and affection and who have given me so much and changed me by their presence in my life, I would need a whole book just to remember them and name all their gifts they shared with me and by which I was blessed.

Author, artist and psychotherapist, Ruth Ghio, aka Beverly Leach, has lived her life in various parts of Northern California where she raised her four children. Finally she settled in Grass Valley, California, where she has lived and worked for the past thirty-seven years. Her life-long commitment to helping others explore the deepest parts of themselves as the surest road to healing has likewise brought her to her own self-awareness and acceptance. These are her stories. She is been here on this planet for 82 years. This is her first book.

CPSIA information can be obtained at www.ICGtesting.com
Printed in the USA
BVOW04s1931101114

374078BV00003B/8/P